T0193961

Hold On To Your Tree : How It Started

An Eye Opener

ROOT
CHALLENGE
INSPIRATION
ASPIRATION
PURPOSE

Claudia Elaine Kellier

authorHOUSE®

AuthorHouse™
1663 Liberty Drive
Bloomington, IN 47403
www.authorhouse.com
Phone: 1 (800) 839-8640

Non-Fiction

Scriptures are taken from the King James Version of the Bible - Public Domain

Published by AuthorHouse   01/25/2018

ISBN: 978-1-5462-1391-8 (sc)
ISBN: 978-1-5462-1389-5 (hc)
ISBN: 978-1-5462-1390-1 (e)

Library of Congress Control Number: 2017916119

Print information available on the last page.

This book is printed on acid-free paper.

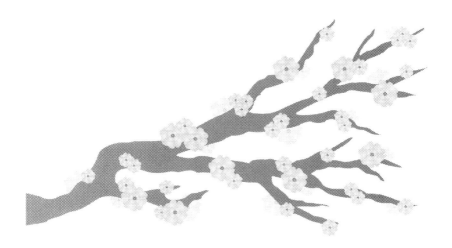

Contents

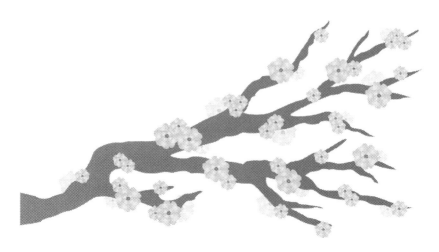

For my children

Diana, Sachelle, Karla, Shari, Janet (step-daughter), Steve (step-son) and grandchildren Saige, Skylar, Christina.

To all

Parents, educators, and especially those who toiled and carried the torch of understanding, morality, good-naturedness and persistence. The staff, parents and well-wishers, too numerous to mention; that sacred preparatory school on the hill that my daughter attended, kudos! I was deeply encouraged by that group to make a difference and to find answers.

Preface

I was lured with exuberance upon making the decision to share not only my educational journey, but my experiences and the satisfaction that I garnered. Also, for being one of those parents who paid keen attention to the involvement and attitude of my daughter Karla, during her first 5 years at prep school. I recognized that during and after school; there were moments which seemed undesirable and those moments basically held her hostage in her own behaviors which became troublesome for both herself and the school environment. In the process of finding answers I embarked on an educational journey which was simply told to the best of my memory.

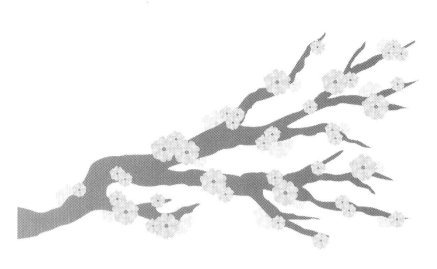

Message

Parents do not ignore indirect messages from your child/children.
Children need to know that parents can be
inspired by them and by doing
so, it can ultimately bring out that potential
which is hidden. Parents,
realize your dream be vigilant.
The constant capricious encounter with my child
catapulted the root of a doctoral journey that timely grew
and transitioned through the timely search for answers
to her innocent plea. I paid attention and I listened
I never had the slightest clue that I had the
ability and the interest to reach
this level. I underestimated my potential to be in
the less than 2% in the nation; according to the
Educational Attainment Census Bureau.

Just imagine! This was propelled and
deeply ignited by the burning
and heartfelt desire to make a difference
just by paying close attention to
and acting on behalf of my own child.

Acknowledgement

Let me first acknowledge the Will of my Creator, who gave me the Wisdom, Knowledge, and the Understanding (WKU). The Patience which is considered a Virtue and the Self-Confidence.

My husband, children, family, friends, and all parents, guardians, educators, and children out there. Be encouraged by my efforts to seek answers to the silent questions and the visible concerns in the eyes of a child.

My grandparents, who throughout their lifetime, have helped to instill the most admirable values in me. I can attest to the tower of strength that I have mustered; which I boast on account of my values.

I owe much to my Publishers for the introduction, encouragement, and support, to enable the process of fast-forwarding renewed interest and alacrity to proceed with this project.

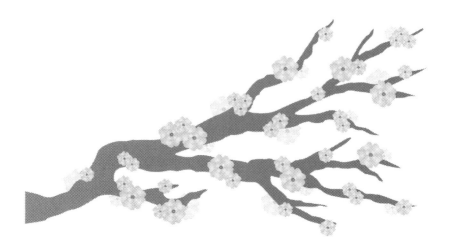

My profound gratitude to my dear mother who is alive and well and my dear father who is deceased, to my mentors and observers, to all those who have touched my life directly and indirectly.

THANKS

About the Author

My name is Claudia Elaine Kellier, I was born in January, a kind hearted, proud, shy; but assertive, observant, non-judgmental and progressive motivator. Third of seven children, a wife, a mother, stepmother, grandmother, aunt. Slow to anger, relies heavily on the map of self-sufficiency, a devoted Christian who depends heavily on Christian principles. I am an Educator, a Researcher, a Guidance Counselor, a Motivator, a Leader, and a Cosmetologist.

I have been through many of life's challenges which provided the life-long learning that helped to propel me to the level where my dreams, anticipation, aspirations, and self- expectations, have been realized as life's challenges removed the shadow that masked self-doubts and limitations. This perpetuated the indomitable mission:-destined for the highest and the determination to reach others with the aim of helping to bring out the best in those lives that I am honored to touch.

Introduction

Drastic action taken to address a root problem
contributed to the growth of an academic threshold
that challenged the ability of a parent to act.
This phenomenon! Theoretically, amounted to a
literal rhetoric likened to an oxymoron such as;
an unpleasantly - challenging scenario pleasantly
skyrocketed an academic reality. The source of the
journey began with the challenge which formed the
root and truly an eye opener; when the growth of an
educational tree was realized.

It all started with one root that was nurtured into an enormous tree.
The eclipse of a mother's instinct with a child's innocent-silent plea at
the age of no more than 5 years. The sulks, the reluctant bewildered,
insubordinate, and extreme defiance, plunged me into a state of
confusion and awe-inspired. I was in a state of "rhetorical-ascension"
the questions were many, mountainous and internal, I had to find

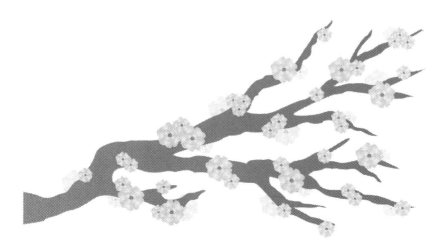

answers but, 'where do I start?' The questions kept flowing. I had to sigh, yes! Many times, over and over until voluntary and involuntary sighing seemed to have clammed into a partial pastime reaction and though they seemed very trifling! I was burdened. I had to find my very own answers as the questions erupted in my head like a volcano, the twist and turns of my own thoughts shadowed me with confusion. I was utterly convinced at that moment in time that action superseded ignorance, a nonchalant attitude to the innocent-silent plea of my child surly would destroy a root that was meant to be.

The Eye Opener

I stopped in my tracks when I was summoned on numerous occasions to the school that my child attended back then; "This is too much, I reckoned to myself, too many times, enough is just enough." I was bombarded by calls from the principal of the school that my child was sometimes uncooperative and a bit unsettled, I knew something was off and I braved the fears that were so obvious but confusing. I applied the brakes on my conceivable independence and everything I had my hands on came to a halt. It was then that my focus was diverted to a different direction from the normal course in my life at that time.

I had a gut feeling that something was building up but could not conceive a root in the making that would open a whole new world in the lives of many; from a single root. All cares were cast on nurturing an inconceivable root. A root, that festered from the experience of a child's educational pathway. A pathway that totally meandered like tributaries moving towards the sea to end its course, so did my child's challenge form this root that totally meandered into the tree that was never imagined. The course of a parent's future had generated. The

complaints from my daughter's school became more and more frequent, it was likened to a canto; the experience became my chapter and had to be told.

Numerous school visits were made to see how best I could manage the capricious encounters that hammered more and more on my conscience to act. Little did I know, that I was meritoriously positioned for my academic take-off and moreover; would endeavor to arrest the obvious of an educational height that would also allow for the tale of an educational journey. Many apologies were constant and consistent as I genuinely gave to all those persons who were exposed to this misunderstanding- innocent plea from a child. A child who was an above average child and one who just needed someone to understand her academic plight which clandestinely triggered: Numerous hands-off attitudes from adults, fellow students, and even siblings simultaneously.

The writing was on the wall only I could not see it. The struggles of an innocent child who had to live an academic life in a stultified academic atmosphere. It is a fact, that schools must have their restrictions, however; restrictions should include considerations commensurate to: Age, ability, time, and place. Even with restrictions; a child should not be a miss-fit but a 'jolly – holly' addition to the classroom fitted with

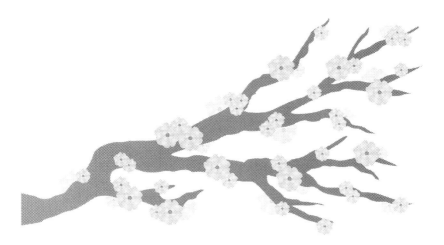

teachers and students and not to be in abeyance to defeat the purpose of active participation. Naturally so, when everything seems fine and one child continues to show discomfort: - concerns are raised. It was in the case of my child who was unable to explain her discomfort but, she expressed it! The best way she could; with very little understanding from those who were in charge and who were expected to mold her young mind.

Careful consideration was not given, by any means, to analyze what was going on in the academic life of this child. It was just not clear why a perfect school system could not see through a child with so little enthusiasm even though whatever restrictive routine there was; it applied to all. To that, 'and I speak loud and clear! No challenges to the system, no disrespect to anyone, no not an iota, and no blame on any rules. The challenge was a child's discomfort and bears no blame on an institution. I struggled with the rhetorical syndrome; answers! Yes, but only to my demise because they never made a difference, the child was the same-frustrated.

I continued to struggle with being patient, undergirded with the struggles of a child who felt the brunt of an 'Adult Misunderstanding Syndrome' (A-M S) i.e., no adult understood the overt rebellion of this

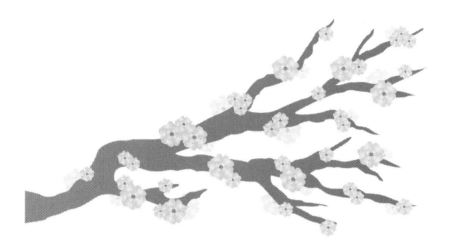

child. Vice versa, an adult who felt the brunt of 'Child-Misunderstanding Syndrome' (C-M S) i.e., the child in the same vain could not understand the adults' uncompromised position. As adults, parent and teachers we refused to compromise our authority and to be subjected to the behavior that was far from silent and unnoticed. For this reason, we were grossly misunderstood by this child and so too we were grossly misunderstood the child.

It took me a few years, to recognize that the delicate 'root' was created and silently nourished as the concerns were never aborted by this misunderstanding rhetoric: - 'Adult-Misunderstanding Syndrome' and the 'Child-Misunderstanding Syndrome'. The constant capricious encounter with my child, catapulted the root of a doctoral journey that timely grew and transitioned through the timely search for answers to an innocent plea from a child. A gut feeling challenged my dear to do nothing about the obvious. Rightly so, I was overwhelmed. I acted out of deep concern for the inevitable.

The imaginable path to finding that behavioral resolve remained grounded in my heart to act and as fate would have it; obscurity was not encouraged, it was not used as an excuse to ignore the nurturing of this tree. This to me, would be enlightened to one who would very well

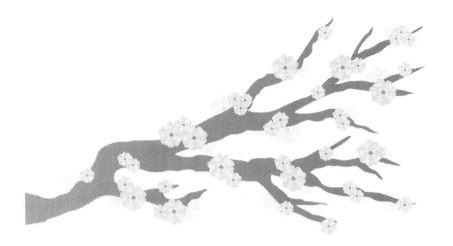

say, 'ignorance of the law gives you the right to commit an offence and punishment consequently', would be an injustice.

I took a very clear and definitive path to nourishing the tree without realizing what the outcome would be. I had no thought and more bluntly! I never tried to understand what it would take for me to find the answers that I needed to alleviate the challenges that I, my child and even the very teachers who thought that she was just a difficult and sometimes defiant student. I started seeking clarifications, opinions, perceptions, advice, incessantly trying to fill a gap which by my own volition was a need and not a choice. The intensity of my search for answers went vertical and horizontal. From the trenchant precipitous brilliance of those who serve as educators, doctors, pastors, psychologists, and those who served as caregivers, friends, relatives and simply those on the periphery of both directions.

My aim was in a bid to find the best answers and to address the plea of my child, I opted for professional advice in earnest as my concerns were many. It was then; I recognized getting to the core of this situation for me, just did not seem like a simple task. As an adult, I misunderstood the reason for the behavior…. So! I constantly tried to change the child's behavior and so did the school. The more I tried the more miniscule the

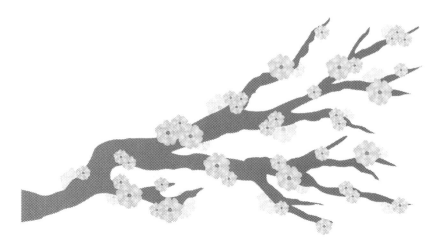

corporation seemed and defiance more noticeable. This attitude surely had a rippling effect as it spilled over into the school environment more and more. I recognized that my understanding of what the child felt was an adult misunderstanding situation. This I considered to myself an Adult-Misunderstanding situation which I, in my own terms considered it a Syndrome; it was a (my) symptom of misunderstanding.

Interpreted this to be an Adult-Misunderstanding Syndrome (A-M S). On the other end of the continuum, the Child-Misunderstanding symptoms I also attributed to the attitude as a symptom of misunderstanding an adult reaction to a situation.

My daughter's syndrome was a misunderstanding of both her mother's reaction and her teacher's reaction toward her. This (C-M S) created the 'Root' and drastic action was the growth of the tree. Challenges had already formed the root and it was one that required the understanding of two syndromes that needed academic ground work /academic search and truth to be told; in a nutshell, was way out of my league and understanding of moving forward.

It seemed quite untenable back then going through the days of the week, as a routine with an innocent child totally dissatisfied and uncompromising as she would tread aimlessly behind me toward the school gate. The unease and

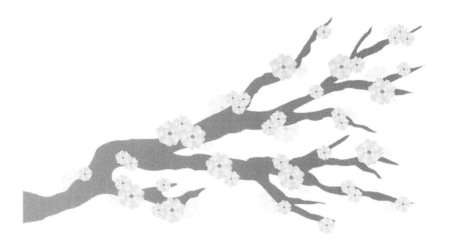

the not so sure attitude crept right into the classroom. The misunderstanding of the child's action was like a border between us as adults and the child and evidently went off track and invariably added to the child's frustration. At the same time, can you imagine what the most obvious thoughts were-going through the child's brain? 'Why! Can't they understand that I am un happy"

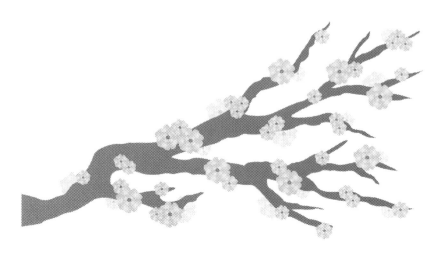

The Journey

The journey began when I realized that enough was really enough. I looked at both scenarios and I recognized that there was so much festering with the challenge of two self-acclaimed syndromes (i.e.) my own interpretation: Adult-Misunderstanding Syndrome (A-M S) and Child-Misunderstanding Syndrome C-M S). My educational journey was put to the test as it started from the root that was 'meant- to- be', however; I was totally oblivious to the fact that my daughter's attitude toward school and my reaction toward the situation would create a scenario that formed the root of my educational journey. The two syndromes encapsulated the kind of unrealistic dream, a trial and error pathway "call it what you may." It is interesting to note that I graduated high school with a piece of paper that showed that I attended high school. Beat that! I ventured into a field that never needed much of an educational armor. I chose cosmetology after I graduated high school and thought it was the end of my journey.

My first school after high school was Leons School of Beauty Culture. The teachers at Leons, they were some of the best and Leons,

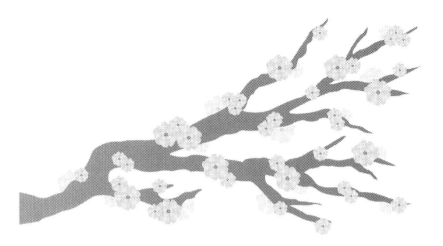

it was the number one school of cosmetology at that time. The teachers? Man! they knew how to disseminate information from the arts and the sciences; which were pertinent to the knowledge that was necessary - for their students to be the best cosmetology professionals. 'A darn good cosmetologist I was too'. With all the skills, I developed; I created a path that was well represented as I worked with the famous and not so famous clients. I was able to hold my own as an entrepreneur back in the day- that was. Life in the field of cosmetology unfolded like the sunflower opening to the days' sun rise in the sky. Oh, how I flourished and yet, in all the splendor of cosmetology I ventured into real estate, car rental and shuttle services. I was in business for the long haul; "at least so I thought".

My focus was financial stability but through it all I considered my options. The time of my life crept on, and on, and on as a business person with no sense of education transformation at any time and at any cost. I realized that with no academic proof of any kind there was the need to do something; however small. I could not boast on being a high school graduate with nothing to show for the years, so, I took it seriously and even though I was vacillating and my thought process in a chatoyant mode - changing like the reflection of bright sun on and off

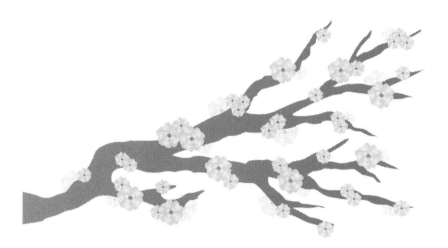

a piece of metal, I went on to making a conscientious move. I registered at a prominent high school in my home town; to join their evening class program where students are being prepared for advance exams which are prerequisites for colleges. Ha! Sounds very strange? Yes, maybe so, I mastered my exams and again told myself I was satisfied with just the strip of paper as proof that I sat the exams and the certificates for my exam passes. I felt a sense of satisfaction and had no intensions of going any further. As time progressed and I lived my life the best way I could at that moment, something else was taking root. Something that had me bound in distress sometimes annoyance, confusion, and the whys' never stop confronting me. I tried to ignore what confronted me but the root held firm and the tree kept growing, virtually impossible to ignore.

My first taste of higher education

Reluctantly, and by virtue of sublimation I picked up my pen and in all consciousness; yet! With doubt hovering over my desire and great ambition to clear the air; I prepared an application for that solemn search. The search to get a better understanding of whom and what constitutes the process of teaching and learning.

The silent plea of a learner must be heard and addressed somewhere! Somehow. I thought why this should be any other but me.

Questions that stirred my thoughts were:

- What are the aims and objectives of the learning institution?
- what is the cause of a child's unconventional behavior towards school and those who are there to mold her and the other learners?
- How is fear identified over plain old reluctance?
- Who is responsible for what and why?
- What motivates learning and how are these principles applied?
- What is our responsibility to the learner?

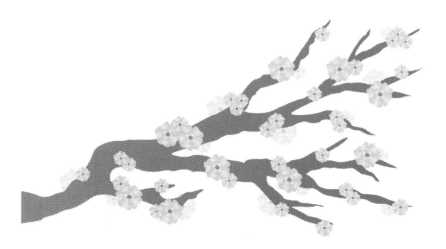

It was also necessary for me to understand what the responsibility of the child was. What is the responsibility of the learner and not just my child?

My questions were numerous and my aim was to bifurcate both syndromes obviously, it was one against the other. I knew somehow that there was a difference between the understanding and concerns of the child and the understanding and similarly concerns of the school. I was fully aware that the challenge was twofold. Even in the midst of deep thinking and searching for the right channel to steer my thoughts I was more confused than I was unconfused.

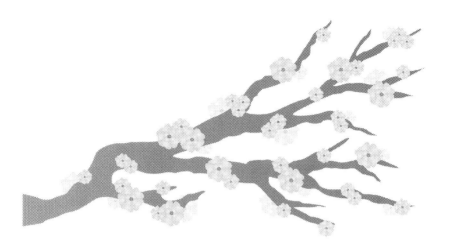

The silent educational anthesis

The journey began in my head and mushroomed as I put my thoughts together. I decided that something had to be done about my child's wellbeing and maybe for others who have or may deem the same fate as I had. Although I had questions before I mailed my college application I felt relieved that I made an attempt to do something that would make a difference if I succeeded. For some strange reason, I had no doubt that I was on the right track; I felt a wave of relief and at no time felt defeated. You know why? I could not even think otherwise because of my desperation for a solution to the challenge that I had. All I could see was an answer for the child's sake and all who were involved.

I completed my application and I mailed it, yes! I did. My challenges though they seemed insurmountable then – I thought even more, and more about the answers that I needed than the question about the; awh-ha! "College," moment. I asked myself numerous times. 'Am I really serious about teachers' college?' I was quite frantic about the brilliant idea; I must say - but then, I was on a mission. I anxiously awaited a response from the college week one…no response, week two….no

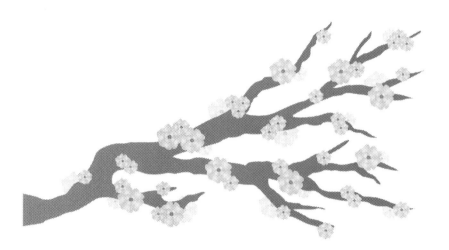

response, week three.....no response. My anxiety faded as I thought less and less about the idea of going to college being a mother of four.

A few weeks had passed and I put the thought of college behind me. Still pondering over my decisions, and the challenges at hand questions continued to surface. One of which was how to meet the need of a child laboring with the dreaded school blues which was obvious. I tried my best to understand what my child and I were up against and amidst trying to fathom the best way forward, I knew something had to give.

I exercised my patience and did the obvious which was to wait. I prayed, and asked the LORD to guide me through it all. My revelation was the Psalms. "I waited patiently for the Lord; and He inclined unto me and heard my cry" (Psalms 40).

I received a letter from the college just when I was settled in my heart that the way forward was in the reply to the application I had sent. I repeated in the silence of my own heart, 'Lord whatever the response is I will be satisfied'. My stentorian response drew the attention of those who were standing by me. The mettle was at hand. With the letter in my possession I looked up and I just whispered a few words which were 'this is it my Lord'. I anxiously opened the envelop and timely read, Yes! I shouted and the rest can be imagined. A momentous journey has begun.

The Message

Dear applicant: Please be advised that your
application for the secondary education program has
been approved…. The date for your interview is….
That was enough for me.

The first unexpected chapter started in my life when this grandiloquent notice hit my eyes, I was flabbergasted. That was the first evidence of the tree steadily moving from its root. Little did I know that the discomfort of my own child's school experience had secured a root that would grow into a tree that I had to prepare myself to secure and nourish as it grew. Upon recognizing that the search for answers were on the horizon; reflections of the growth of my educational journey flashed across my mind's eyes many times over, I carefully and secretly made the necessary preparations to secure my place in earnest- pursuit of this venture. My greatly appreciated acceptance to teachers' college sure was an anchor which my memoir will reveal. I immediately promised

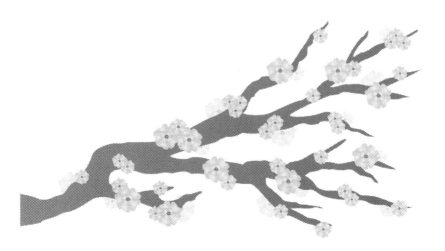

myself that I would Spear no stops in preparation for this unexpected and coveted opportunity.

I carefully went through the list that was prepared for me as a new student and smiled as I breathed deeply in and out and with every breath that I took in and let out - I whispered, "Thank you Lord, thank you Lord". I broke the news and every family member were in a state of shock.

No one knew I made that move. The secret of it all was a matter of choice as my family both immediate and extended would have thought that I was at a different level of crazy. With that said; lucky for me, I was at that level of crazy. The night had fallen and I retired to bed. No questions asked, no comments made; which was to my surprise. Why this was so, no one took me serious. However, I told my daughter who was responsible for my teachers' college decision that I was intent on nurturing the root she had created. I assured her that she would see and enjoy the benefit from the growth as answers I would surely find. Too young to understand what I meant, but! She was the initiator and I forged ahead because I wanted to help my child who unknowingly by her unease literally forced the effort that I mustered to have taken the bold step.

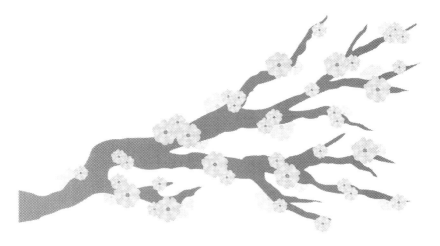

The anxiety and anticipation of college made me restless that night. I was up at the crack of dawn and ready to take on the responsibility that had afforded me. I felt honored, and I did myself justice; I convinced myself that it was truly so. Ha! as I counted the hours to the opening of all the stores where I could purchase all the items that I would need in preparation for college. I secured all the items that I needed for college before I even went for my interview. I knew, within myself, that nothing could stop me again and more-so; for the very reason that I got that far. I was determined more than ever before to be the champion of that cause. That cause! I lamented, and convinced myself that it would determine the growth of that tree. The weeks went by and I counted every minute as I waited for my date to be interviewed. I continued to do my shopping as needed and waited patiently.

The weeks turned into days and the days turned into hours. The day before my interview at the college, I refreshed my memory on several matters relating to the who and the why of my mission. I had everything in place for the moment. The interview date had finally arrived. I was up that glorious morning very early. I gave thanks to my Creator for making that day possible and also for continued guidance and favor. I prepared myself adequately and was confident that I had all

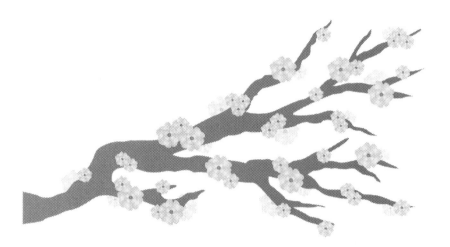

the prerequisites needed for the occasion. I made my way to the college which is situated on a hill with the most magnificent view of the city. As I climbed the hill slowly in my car I felt a tinge of unease. I made it to the top of the hill and found a place to park and as I parked the car a very strange feeling came over me as the number of interviewees mounted by the minute, on the college campus. Their reason was the same as mine was.

Preparation for Teachers College

The interview

In the year 1997

The little groups were scattered all over the college campus. It was quite clear that anxiety was hovering over all the little groups as there was so much gesticulation that could not go unnoticed, the hands were moving up, down, sideways, and even wrist movements as if they were waving goodbye. Some individuals were pacing the spot where they were standing as if they were in an exercise class with strict instructions to do so. Some persons were just staring into space, whereas, some were clutching on to the arms of others as to say "I am nervous, are you nervous too? I was not close enough to hear the words going back and forth but, body language in times like those that I experienced, did say a lot.

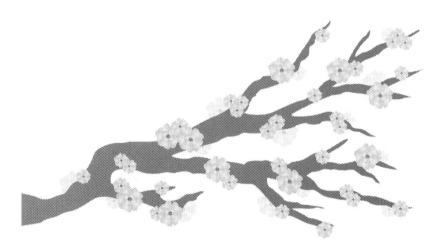

I was a loner basically; I only said hello to those closes to me as I walked by observing where my many hours and days would be spent for the next three years. As I strolled around and admired the campus, I thought of being on the college campus and how I would fit in much more than I thought about the interview that I would be going into at that moment. The time drew closer and all those who were on the outside were summoned on the inside of the very hugh auditorium that was prepared for the purpose. I took my seat; so too, did everyone else. I gazed around the auditorium but the object that caught my eyes the most was the college crest that was strategically placed on the wall in full view for everyone to observe. I gazed steadily at the crest on the wall and I made a vouch at that very moment. I silently told myself that I would never walk down that hill until my reason for the moment is accomplished.

I was moved psychologically both vertically and horizontally. I felt success and I felt passion. I was so moved by the fact that I was on a college campus waiting to be interviewed; something that was never in my repertoire. That moment, I never saw even in my wildest dream. "To God Be the Glory." I was so confident that day, I had no time to get those flapping butterfly feelings in my stomach nor could I wonder

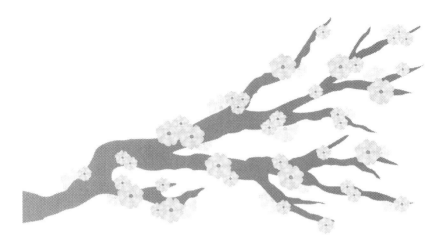

off any further in my mind, I had to pay attention now as persons were being summoned to various areas for their interview. It was then, only then, that I paid attention to the real moment. Anxiety kicked in and the questions flashed swiftly across my mind and they were many. I asked myself if I was totally prepared for the mission ahead. I never answered the question but! What I knew was that my mind was made up.

It was my time eventually. I was ushered to the adequately spaced area where anxiously awaiting interviewers welcomed me and introduced themselves before offering me a seat. I was interviewed by the principal and a few others who asked me the obvious questions. I was asked questions like why I chose that institution and that area of study and how will I use my training to benefit both myself and the education process…just to name a few of the questions asked. In the interview, there were also a few concerns that were shared by both parties, most of them were clarified. The questions asked by the interviewers were relevant and fair enough to the interviewee. I answered the questions and expressed my concerns also. I felt confident that I would be among the number of students walking through the doors of this very noble institution; come August Morning.

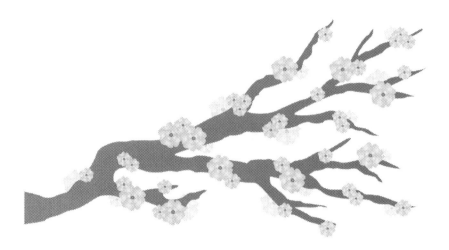

"Thank you! Lord, for this opportunity" I must have said a hundred times to myself during the interview as I observed the expressions and the overall body language of the interviewers, my confidence kept rising. I had no doubt in my mind that I would be further contacted and so too, I had no doubt that the further contact response would be a favorable one. While the team deliberated as to whether there were any other questions or concerns, I held my breath many times over with an attempt to manage my composure which I did. I did so with all the air I could muster before exhaling silently. My chest lowered without any notification of the breathing relaxation exercise that I was doing while they reasoned to them. In no time, I heard the thank you for considering this institution and for making the interview. I was further assured that I would be informed of the team's final decision at the earliest possible date.

I, somehow maintained my composure, gave a smile and expressed my share of appreciation to all members of the team. I secured my documents and other accompaniments that I had and steadily walked out of the office. I kept smiling because I knew right there and then that there was a place for me on that campus. I chit-chatted a bit with others who were also doing their share of chit-chatting and rightly so, we

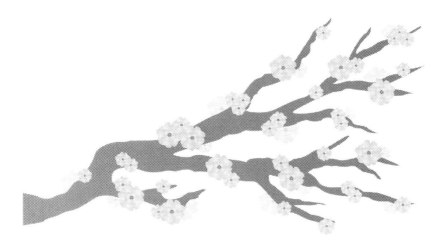

all felt a level of confidence. I went to my car and made my way down the hill on the campus grounds. I went home and as the days went by, I continued with my usual daily engagements and waited patiently. As anyone else would have done; I counted the minutes, the hours, and the days with circles of thoughts, depth of anticipation, and even width of emotions and questions, and to a great extent my own answers that may not have made much of a difference or even relevance to my situation. However, all thoughts were still accommodated until the day I received the letter from the college.

That very day, I clearly remember; when I looked to the Heavens as if I was about to take a few steps up. My fingers moved across the envelope like they were playing the keys on a piano and my head fixed upright into the sky. I breathed a silent prayer. "Thank you, my Lord, and Savior." Yes! That was my prayer. I anxiously opened the envelop and alas! I sure was right, I was definitely in the number as I expected. Again, I got busy, busier than before I got my telephone out and I called up my seamstress, shared with her the marvelous news. She congratulated me and before I could say another word, she said, "Bring the uniform pattern and the material and I will get right into action so you can be ready for your big day." I agreed and before the

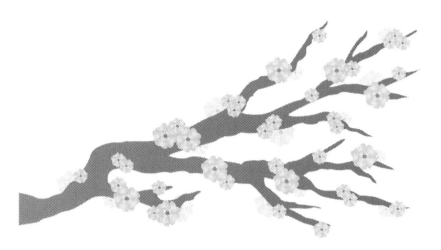

day was done I was in my seamstress's apartment with my material and uniform pattern. The school's uniform was a choice of three colors for the blouse: White, sky blue, and baby pink. There was also a choice between dark blue and khaki for skirts and slacks. She hastily took my measurements and wished me well as she moved her tape measure over all the areas of my body that she needed to secure my measurement for building the uniforms accurately for my stature. I told her thanks and smiled as I left her apartment knowing that she would do a marvelous job on the tunics.

My next agenda, was, to secure the proper shoes for the extra strides that I would be doing on the college compound. That was not a problem as there were many comfortable ones to choose from in the stores. I went on to gathering all other materials that I needed for the start of the school year. I read my acceptance letter a million times over. I went through the list that I had no less; just to make sure that I had everything listed on the paper. I was satisfied with my progress and gave myself a break on the college demands. My regular routine was continued until the sacred Sunday that preceded the long-awaited Monday morning.

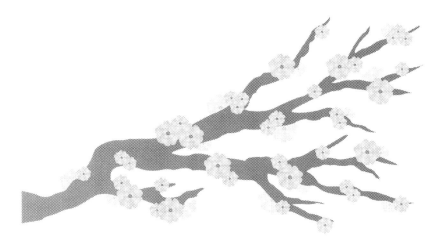

I had picked up the uniforms from the seamstress a week prior to that Sunday before classes would begin. That Sunday! was a very special one. It was not just another day for regular church, because the anticipation of the very next day was packed into it in so many ways. I tried the uniforms so many times that I had stop counting how many. I dressed myself completely a few times and surely, I was pleased. The rest of the Sunday went by and then came the day for the real test. Orientation was scheduled to begin that Monday at 9 o'clock sharp so I timed and paced myself carefully.

I anticipated the anxiety; not just for myself, but also for my family members too. After all - they too! were going to be greatly impacted by my new schedule and commitment. It was a choice that I made and hoped that by so doing it would also be of great benefit to all who were impacted by the challenges we had and continued to endure. Did I do the right thing? I convinced myself that drastic action had to be taken and this was what it meant. Education!

Monday morning! I shouted, as the feeling of the transforming factor hit solidly on my academic aspirations; totally generated by a child. I rose at the first sight of day break which was no later than 5am eastern.

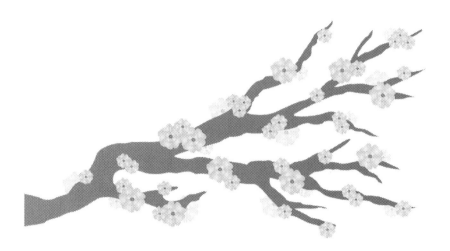

I knew that it would be a challenge but I already programmed my mind and assured myself that I would drag with me three things 1. Perseverance, 2. Resilience, 3. Determination. I had a child to take to school which had to fit into my schedule. Fortunately for me, there was something called early learning sessions. As much as she was turned off from school most times, I encouraged her and even with much reluctance she would comply. I took her to school many times with sadness in my own heart but I found comfort knowing that I was trying to answer her call for help. I made myself coffee, did my early morning chores and then made our breakfast; I managed to get both ourselves ready for the day and left home early enough to be free from the heavy traffic going in our direction daily.

I got on to the college campus at 8 o'clock am, and to my amazement, the entire lot of familiar faces that I had seen the day of the interview; were very well present. We congratulated each other and made ourselves comfortable in the auditorium as there were signs strategically placed with very precise instructions as to how all interviewees would proceed. At 8: 45 am, all who were responsible for orientation took their positions, the auditorium that sounded like a beehive up to the hour of 8: 40 am, became silent. At 8: 55 am, I

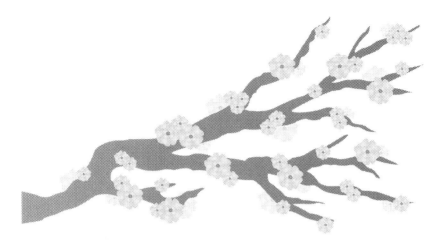

heard the blurting sound from the microphones and then a loud voice from the orientation coordinator 'Good morning everyone, welcome to the Sam Sharp Teachers College......' At the end of the welcome all academic and administrative staff were introduced to all attendees.

The principal spoke, the vice principal spoke, heads of departments and there were a few announcements here and there. From the school nurse, the counselors ect. and all academic and administrative staff members were involved in the orientation process. The process went on for a few days and in the process the seniors did their share of grubbing us the new comers. Much of the grubbing was ridiculous and annoyed me greatly but this was a part of being a first year.

At the end of the orientation everyone knew where they were placed, who their instructors were, all heads of departments, the tuck shop, music room, main hall, staffroom, dorms, nurses station and offices. All attendees were prompted for questions and concerns and there were many.

At the end of the orientation all parties seemed satisfied, and then came the break. We were scattered all over familiarizing ourselves with areas that we were given the authority to occupy. The feeling of ownership on a college campus made me realize that my mountain of

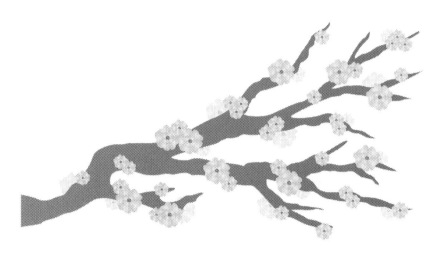

success which I truly attributed to my daughter could not be built by anyone but myself.

I positioned myself in my mind; for way beyond the following Monday when classes would begin. The days occupied with orientation practices went well and so did the rest of the week. The weeks went by and the months went by and so did the years. My challenges in between were many but I lived by one thing (The Word). As the Good Book says "In the Beginning the Word was with God." As an ardent believer in the Word, I feasted my inner thoughts on many; as a matter of fact, one of my pastimes was the reading of the Psalms.

It took me no time to recognize that my mountain of success could not be built by anyone but me, this understanding nestled me in times of bewilderment when tough decisions were my barriers. There were times when I felt overwhelmed by like my feet were caught in a net and I remember Bet Moore's words when she delivered her message and reminded her listeners of the (The Word). The Word from the Psalm stated: "He will pluck my feet from out of the net," again from (The Word) Psalm 25 Verse 15, which assured me that when my eyes are forever kept on the Lord I would be set free. I cleared all doubt and tried to remain calm and focused. My academic journey was not just

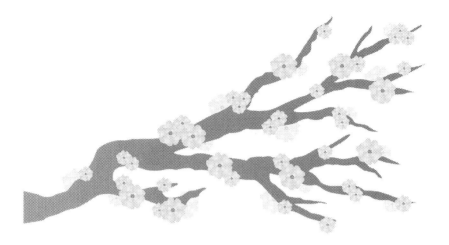

a simple one and I was quite aware, all I knew was that I had a child who needed help and I was convinced that if not myself, then who, who could I depend on to find the answers. Every day was like a dream and for the first year in college I looked at myself many times in the mirror with my full college attire and without asking the same questions that I often regenerate, I just give myself one answer. Believe in yourself and continue to strive valiantly and again (The Word). I repeated many times, "I can do all things through Christ who strengthens me."

I refused to allow procrastination to violate my progress and I made the conviction that resilience, perseverance, and determination would be my back pack with everything that followed me each day. My first-year journey was a very tedious one, lecturers were very professional and did ever thing they could to assist the students, all academic staff were very accommodating except for those who had their favorites and thought that some students were more equal than some were, administrative staff were easy to reach. Again, can't get away from the favoritism syndrome.

Classes were good notwithstanding the rigors of getting it all in and the testing and the exams were brain busting. There was a cloud of selfishness to contend with as some students were very clannish and if you were not conducting yourself a certain way, believe it! You would

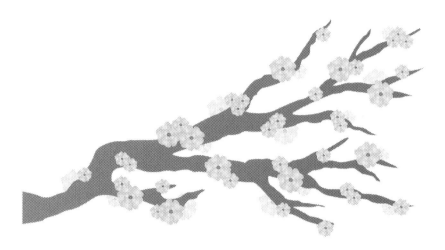

not be lucky enough to get any assistance from them, not to mention simple information if you needed it. Those were some of the escapades of first year that I had experienced. In all fairness, I survived it and I am grateful. It surely was a Blessing for me when I chose Guidance and Counseling as my major in college. Psychology had me grounded as I had to cover the areas that dealt with psychological development, behaviors, and learning.

Psychology was very challenging for me, so too was Classroom testing and measurement, other subject areas were not easy, but! those two areas stood out most for me at the time. The year ended with final exams which were well done. However; I was not successful at the first sitting of the dreaded Classroom Testing and Measurement. I had to do a re-sit before the end of the school year for me to graduate at the end of the third year. The second time around and bingo! Hey! I made it. I learnt one thing; you can never be considered a failure until you fail to try again. Psychology taught me how to manage the fear of failure.

College in the first year was like moving into a new neighborhood and having to meet and make new friends. Some neighbors welcome you, some neighbors have no care at all who you are being in their space, some quiet and conservative, some more on the noisy side, some treat

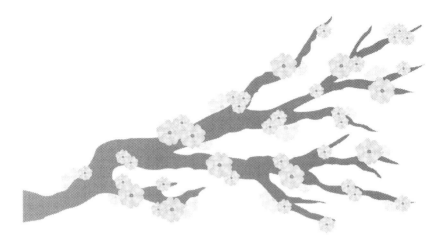

you like family and invite you over, some entertain with their hi! And hello! But keep their distance. At the end of the day college is one big family no matter what differences we had. The great experiences that I had in year one, I would not trade it for anything. I survived.

Moments of Change

College was famous for social gathering and etiquette was just as imperative. The school's cafeteria was both the formal and informal area and was visited religiously at every lunch break; it was always interesting as the grandiloquent appearance of the principal could not be missed during those periods. I cannot forget the rigors at lunch time when the principal would walk into the lunch area and made sure that all students were dining as if lunch time was the formal occasion of the school day. Backs had to be straight and knives and forks properly used.

It was very surprising see that there was so much focus on dining but, social etiquette that took precedence at the beginning of year one - by the time some students got to year two they dropped the skill. Little did I know that the principal was aware of this and sacked the inappropriateness of dismantling social graces. She noted that the present moment was the opportune time when they should put it into practice and pass it on to the very students that they would someday serve.

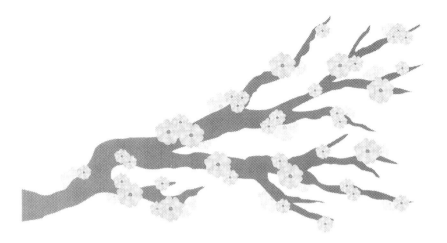

That lesson was surely a direct hit on my consciousness. I realized that many important things that seemed insignificant in year one and were brushed off; they were some of the elements needed to form the basic substance of the educational foundation. Many students thought it was a crazy idea for paying attention to the little things but, to be honest; it made sense! The little deeds of morality rejected day by day may one day see the rise of a nihilistic practice. Remember! Psychology groomed me, I was well taught in year one. These were some of the little moments that cemented many chains of thought and made me realize why the social graces; were ignored in many areas.

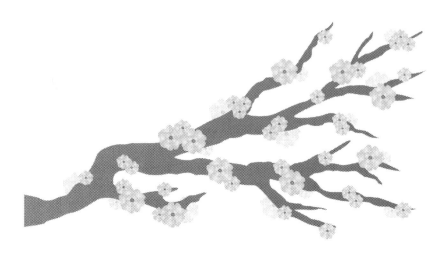

Act of Charity

The college catered to special occasions for the aged and the more vulnerable citizens in the community. Students would go out and assist and some would play their part on the grounds of the college to accommodate these folks. It was special moments like those that drew me even closer to being there for others, it also helped me to better understand what life is worth. I went in search of behavioral misunderstanding, little did I know that there were numerous and desperate needs to be met and they were right there at the same place; teachers' college. This act of kindness was a tradition of the college which the principal held dear to her heart.

Some students took away much from the experiences with these groups and some took nothing. As for those who took nothing, it was just another way for the college to place unnecessary burden on students from years one two and three. Some students were happy that they had the opportunity to serve those less fortunate and felt privileged that they could put brilliant smiles on their faces.

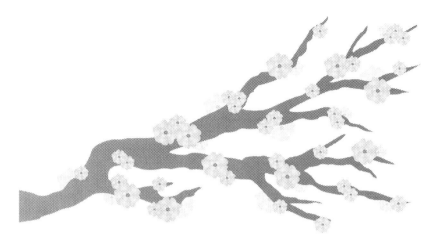

Metaphorically speaking; college in year one had many faces. Learning took place in so many ways and it took me days and weeks to fathom, 'why? Why just why! Do some individuals chose the teaching and learning route. For some students; it was like a dream come through. Some appeared to be a coerced unintentional venture. Some were observable attitude were as if; who cares, just something to do. As for me, it was nothing short of a miracle. However, in many instances, I wondered to myself – no pun intended, what constituted some of those dreams that flooded the institution. One thing was common, despite the many faces of college in year one the charitable moments had one face. They were embraced by all. I, tentatively tried to manage my emotions which ran wildly like tributaries entering the ocean and notably undulating as my mood and energy went up and down. I tried my best not to conform to my outward reaction but therefore; to manage the college scenario and at the same time my own child's emotions – as she greeted her learning environment daily.

Teachers were challenged too, they also had to play their part by making their contribution to the school's charitable activities. Throughout my learning experience I asked the question, 'who or what strikes the balance? Year one was one that can never be forgotten.

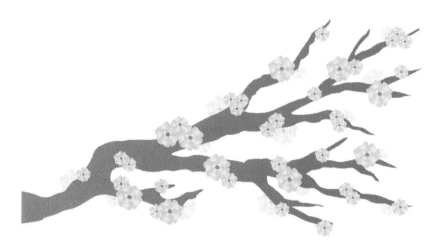

The level of socialization, participation, and understanding of the: Technical, social, and academic world – at a different level, was the first pace that regimented my academic awakening. This academic awareness concretized a mindset that prepared my aspirations and beliefs at a level that could never be lowered. Year one! Was the pace setter. I moved forward knowing that endurance was factored into my academic race and my mission was to serve.

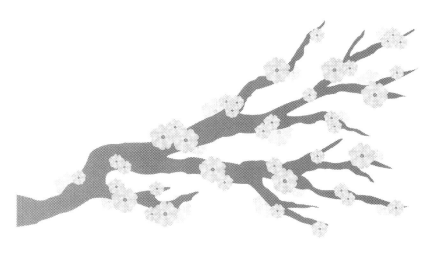

Second Year

The college year started with much enthusiasm. I made it to a second year, some students did not. Oh! How good I felt to have made it back. I was on top of any cloud; as you can imagine. I reiterated the first Monday morning I took my daughter to school and before I dropped her off I reminded her that going to teachers' college was not my idea, it was hers. I was doing so because I needed to find the most suitable way to help her with her struggles and I decided to test the system that prepared the educators who were there to mold her young mind.

I dropped her off at school that morning once again as I did before in year one. I kept looking back at the routine that I had in year one and recognized that it was another year of the same. I continued my merry way for my first taste of college life as a second-year student. It was the same routine and the same story in my daughter's ears except that I was getting closer to my goal. The same preparations that were made for year one were also made for year two in addition to the year two requirements. My demanding responsibilities were no less - in any way, they were even more to tackle for the journey.

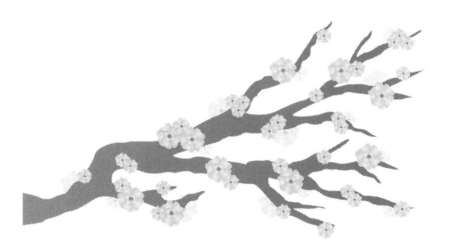

I had prepared myself mentally and physically during the break between years one and two. I had everything that I needed by then and was ready for the year two, school year. I had somehow mastered the art of allowing the challenges to only affect me to the extent that I allowed them to do so. Psychology taught me how? It sure did. Surely, I knew those (challenges) and many more would surface. I had also learnt enough psychology from the famous Psychologist: Burrhus Fredric (B.F.) Skinner, to not pay much attention but to understand it by looking at the causes of the actions that confronted and what the consequences were. This knowledge backed me back me up in so many instances of both college and personal life.

I had to be creative in finding the most desirable responses to introduce when I observed where behaviors needed to be modified. I was better equipped to handle the day to day affairs of all my children and their:

Actions, emotion, and thoughts. However, my target was the "root" my child's cry for help. The focus was! And I say was! Because! It was the concerns of one child that forced me into finding solutions to the challenges of learning and how to effectively manage. I felt quite confident after my first year knowing that I had become the changed

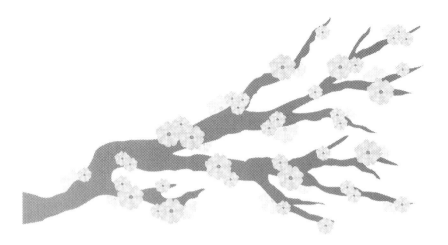

agent. Second year was similarly enlightening; there was no less of an opportunity to be casual and formal in the same setting. The school's lunch area was the formal area and was visited religiously at every lunch break; it was always interesting as nothing changed from the first year where the grandiloquent appearance of the principal could not be missed during those periods. Year two was just an extension of year one with more: Depth, expectations, dedication, application, independence, commitment, greater focus and understanding of who we were and where we were going and why.

These phenomenal attributes, psychology taught me how important they were and how to apply them not- only for personal actualization but to others also. Lectures, both the old ones from year one and the new ones in year two were very supportive and clearly understood our struggles and concerns. They were always willing to accommodate us whether our concerns and attentions were directly or indirectly or if they themselves were assigned to us directly or indirectly. They were phenomenal! Clear instructions and information were always available to all; college resource were more than adequate.

Social life in college was never limited, but then, I was a mother of four! Therefore; I really missed out on much of college social life and

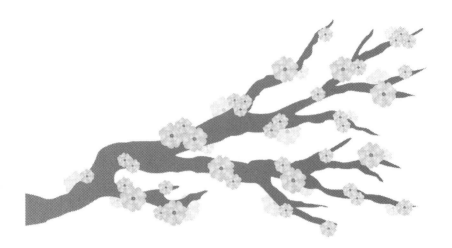

entertainment. I was always the first one to exit the lecture halls. Not because I was a bad student but my responsibilities never allowed me much room to sit and waver about the lecture or anything for that matter. Notwithstanding; my commitment to college was well cemented. My commitment to the reason why I was there in teachers' college from the onset was strong enough to alleviate any fear of failure. I paid my dues in every possible way. All I needed was to maintain my concentration skills and apply them at all cost. The college's grandiloquence was a natural part of college life for all students.

College activities demanded a natural reflex action where students move towards college activities without having to give any serious thought to the process or events. Unfortunately, for me, I was not as flexible. My natural reflex action was to head down the hill at the sound of the last bell. Most times I had school pick up to do on Fridays. I had to travel out of town to another parish many miles away to the boarding school where I had two children attending school and Yes! I had to do the work.

Second year was a trying time no less than first year which I admit was a tedious task but, 'hello, we all knew it was inevitable, cannot get to second without going through first, can we? Well! 'Yes', I remembered

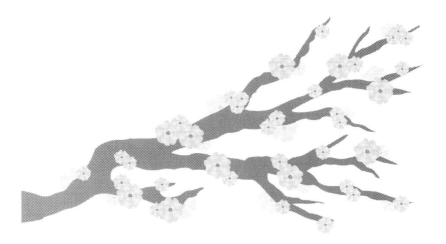

two students who joined us in year two as advanced students. Rightly so. For most of us we started from one. My greatest challenge in second year was classroom testing and measurement. Mrs. Clark-hall (not her real name) was an excellent teacher! but for some reason, I was not the mathematical type. Lucky for me, I am an auditory learner and I process information very well when I am attentive, concentrate to my fullest capacity, process the information carefully and remember the most important parts of the spoken words (my assessment and conclusion of active listening).

I was saved many times in my exams because of this active listening skill that I had. Most times it was my note taking strategy; the fine details that I remembered was from listening. I observed that even though us, as learners, we all had one aim – to get out into the education world, however, we were all so different. Some students were like bee hives and very disturbing to the keen listeners. Some students never laid down a pen, it was all scribbling, and some students never seemed to get it without some level of demonstration. I never gave much consideration to the learning diversification as a student in high school; it never seemed significant until I reached college.

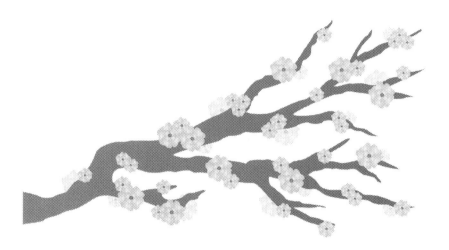

First year was the year when I worked hard to cover all the courses, I dug very deep into the process of understanding the learner and tried hard to apply what I covered during that period in my desperation. Some questions were: What are the parameters of learning? Who is the learner and how does learning take place? I searched hard to and tried my utmost to also understand the aims and objectives of the learning process and those who serve in all capacities of the learning. I could cypher the multiplicity of characters that I had around me at the time.

Each and every one seemed to have had a very diverse way of structuring various tasks assigned; be it group or individual assignment. The responses weighed heavily on our understanding, requirements, and expectations as it was interesting to note at that time how crucial it was to use analytical skills and how to apply them. For some students,' it was not necessary to carefully analyze tasks assigned and they sure did prove their ability to analyze when they responded to their tasks. Lecturers were many times very puzzled by the actions taken from time -to-time by my classroom colleagues. Their responses were sometimes questionable, and questions that were asked most times in the tutoring sessions, could frankly be considered eminently reasonable. Some! They

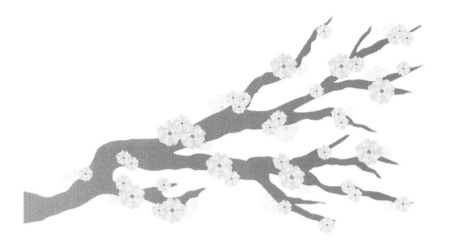

were not so prominent and could be ignored. In any event; it is said that questions were designed to be asked-and- asked, they sure did.

In any event, the experience that I had; 'for me? It was too rich to undervalue... The diversity was interesting and more so connecting with them was even more interesting. I was in an enviable position and did take the initiative to make these connections a memorable one.

I was exposed to all levels of: Creativity, learning styles and abilities, attitudes, likes and dislikes, just to name a few. The learning opportunity was laid before me like a platter full of confectionaries at a party. Believe me! I did feast on all the knowledge that I could muster daily. My major in counseling gave me the edge and the psychological tools to do my own assessment and analysis on most of what I had experienced. As a secondary education guidance and counseling major I welcomed every course that I covered in year one and those that were included in year two.

The second year was much more intense as the depth of psychology and the counseling sessions gave me most of the answers that I needed for myself and my own children. I was also instrumental in helping my own colleagues in college. I had gathered so much in year one and by year two I had developed greater confidence, I must proudly say

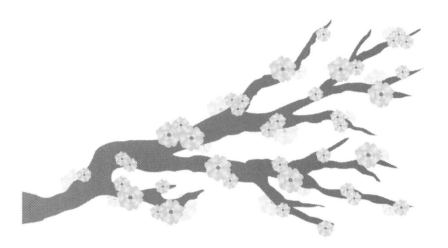

"in myself and my knowledge base." it was a resounding triumph over many of my doubts, it was pretty-much solid. Yes! Based on what I had learnt then and how to put it all into practice. Much of my training were practiced on my home base, there were others outside of college who knew what my college course entailed and sought my intervention in many instances.

It was a great pleasure for me to assist where I could.

Year two went by despite the constant hitches in my personal, social and college life. Many times, there were tussles with group assignments, individual course grades, tutors seemingly leaning toward some more than others. Friends parted with friends and were left behind unpopular in many cases as the ones who were the popularity – magnets by their own volition; had created their own clique. Some students absquatulate from groups and even their friends so many times that as a result-acquaintance were left in a quandary and more importantly many group activities suffered in the process. By the end of the school year, the group dynamics was prevalent as preferences manifested - just a few of the hiccups, minor they were, but let's face it perceptions were running high and wide. Though there were many frustrating moments in both first and second years, the good outweighed the evils. College activities

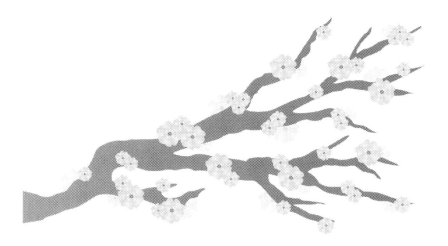

were many, all students had to be involved in social clubs and societies and active credible community associations.

Second year students had to commit themselves to taking on first year students as little brothers and sisters and be their mentors. I had my share of struggles managing my own affairs being a fulltime family woman who: - by the understanding of some husbands; should have no business in school after they are married. Those students who were married and had children; they were very supportive of the ones who were more vulnerable being wives and mothers and tried to keep up with being students. The task was tedious the journey seemed endless but the goal was in sight. There were those persons who touched my life in so many ways they will always be in my repertoire of friends; they will always be remembered for their kindness.

My principal in college at that time was a real gem and a true inspiration especially in times of uncertainty. She guided me through the academic path that I took and encouraged me daily. My counselors were like my parents; they were very supportive, nonjudgmental, took no excuses where they were not necessary, always encouraging and guided my academic path in many ways. Their intervention helped me to manage my challenges as they surfaced in many and different

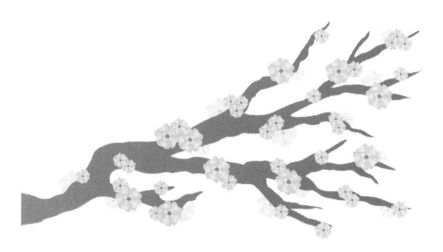

ways. My learning trajectory was very dynamic and connected in three dimensions, i.e. the hard, the soft and the mild way.

I could understand that:

'When life throws, a ball find a progressive – resilient
bat, when life shoots a dart always be prepared with
a determination-dart board, when life shoots you an
arrow your perseverance-shield will back it off'.
(My own interpretation and my focus).

Being discouraged may have been a factor in areas of my life but my lifelong learning trajectory helped to strengthen my focus. I was determined through my challenges that one thing for sure; my goal would never be compromised. The first two years in college gave me a sense of self- preservation and ownership. It took me to a level of psychological independence that removed any possible self-limitation that I had and would seek to encourage. With the mindset that I had, I went on to my third year, in college, with every confidence that success was and would continue to be in my favor.

My Third Year

My only intension was to help my child to adjust to the challenges of school life. I intended to go through the first year of college, gather enough information and fix the challenge that had been festering with my child and school. When I completed first year it was too fascinating to cut short. When I got to the second year it was even more fascinating, I saw myself having meaning to not only help my own child but I saw making a difference globally. First and second years taught me and exposed me to a global and continuous impact in the same way some of the most famous educators and psychologists have contributed globally and with consistency. I was so fascinated with the work of these men and women who paved the way for others like me and many others. The great work that they did, provided me with answers.

My major in guidance and counseling landed me in the path of scholarly circles. The root of a troubled child was the root of a journey that I never saw. Third year! The most dreaded of the three years. By then I had learnt college life to the fullest. I knew who I could lean on, who and what to stay clear of, when to cry or laugh, when to

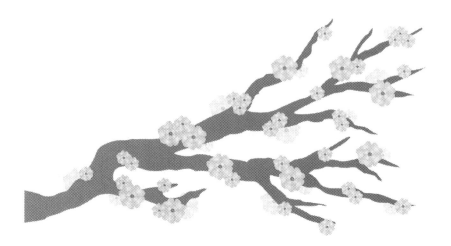

surface and when to hide, when to run and when to walk, it taught me independence, virtues, caring for others, when to stand up, and when to take a seat, when to stay, and when to let go. All the experiences I mention I have lived.

Every iota of them! As a college student, I have experienced all angles. I can recall what Dorothy Height, said about greatness, and I mentioned this because greatness is how we see ourselves within our dreams and aspirations and the way it will make a difference in our lives and the lives of others. She said! "Greatness is not what you accomplish but the opposition that you overcome to reach your goal". It is befitting to ask ourselves the golden question. Do I have a goal, what is my goal; is it achievable, how will I achieve it?

I had innumerable opposition and college taught me how to successfully fight back and overcome to reach my final year, 'the great year three'. The great battle of the course work, the clubs and societies, other college activities and numerous social interventions and interactions. Year three was that year when the focus was on final exams, all students tried their best to shy away from college activities so that they could focus all their attention and energy on their exams. The college academic and administrative leaders would have none of

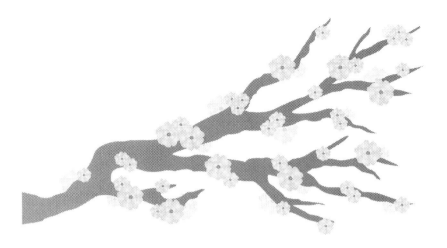

that however; there were many more like me who was not able to give their usual support to these activities. I must admit; yet, I am not at all proud to say that my social involvement was not a very consistent one throughout my college years.

I was not very active in those areas; college life was a very tight one. My personal life was not one that gave me much of a lee-way so the choice was limited to much social activities.

Going through my third year, in college, I had so many mixed feelings, I was stunned many times but ameliorated in the web of my own feelings as optimism was my driver in all consciousness. I saw the need to make the difference in my own life and in the lives of the others whose path I have trod, those that I presently impact, and those that I have not yet met. I have the propensity to make the adjustment and the connections where necessary in the education system, the opportunity to grow, the determination and the zeal to conquer the fears and doubts that I had about my own self, and my child. I felt many times like I was dreaming and needed a wakeup call to the real world.

There were times when I kept saying to myself, 'I am a student in teachers' college, what a miracle my whole world has changed'. I saw myself in a million different places and positions and the joy of having

my own educational strength to tackle my daughter's aversion to school. It was even more touching! When I reflected on what had initiated the first thought of where to turn for answers. Who, would have thought that it would be from the root of my own child's cry for help. Was this a coincidence or was it an un foreseen miracle? The root of a problem created the root of a journey that landed me in a position which enabled me to be multifaceted. Reverend T.D. Jakes once said that, 'if you seek to be understood you can be confined'. I was on a mission that no one understood; not even myself, all I wanted were answers. I can recall hearing many times that I was difficult and no one could understand me. I was a victim and those words were very troubling to me and on many occasions, I tried my best to appease those very persons who branded me as one who could not be understood.

What I discovered during my training was that understanding someone was not forcing the person to say what you want to hear, or, wanting them to comply with your demands. The essence of understanding someone is when you can appreciate ones: Expression, their level of understanding and communicating, choices, feelings.…… In retrospect, theoretically; Reverend T.D. Jakes, understands that there are many persons who have been and are constantly been confined;

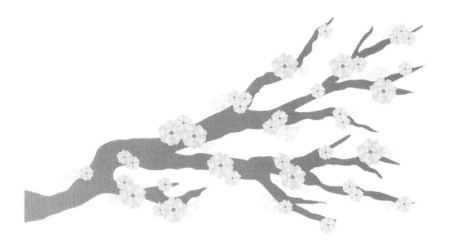

trying hard to opening themselves to Understand others and to be understood by others. My own child, was very much confined because us! Adults. As adults, we wanted her to feel and to be what we wanted from her; for our own comfort and reason. As adults, we could not appreciate the child's own understanding of her little academic world and the very way that she could express herself.

I was a victim and when I understood the whole dynamics of being understood, I became a victor. Throughout my college years I fought through the everyday class assignments, individual and group work, test taking, college activities and again, I was bombarded with my personal responsibilities. I went through my first two years with tears and equally laughter, I was like a typical robot, in college the students called me 'Got to go,' I was always on the move. God knows, how I made it through the first two years and through to the third.

I persevered because I knew that the reason was beyond my understanding. Many times, the challenges which included college expectations seemed insurmountable. The mettle that propelled me through the previous two years was my anchor for the rest of my college year. I persevered with every psychological strength that I never knew I

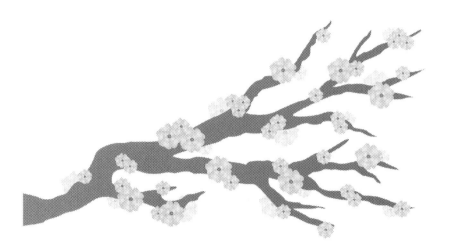

had. I was like a lone ship on the high seas. I was not comfortable with the idea of exposing too much; I was very reserved, not very sociable.

I was a very private person and thought that the challenges of college should remain on college grounds and personal home challenges remain at home. The year, went by very fast and the final year, exams was no easy walkover, it was yet another hurdle and there was no safe anchorage for procrastination, the pendulum would swing one way or the other and the choice was mine and mine alone where it swung.

it was a crucial time for me in multiple ways but I managed to stay the course. I tried my best to make it worth my while as a mother, a wife, and a student. I was proud of myself; I acknowledged my success and graduated a proud mother knowing that I tried to make a difference in the lives of many.

Thanks to all my teachers and friends who saw the need to remain faithful and thanks also to those who bitterly opposed me, it helped to strengthen me in leaps and bounds. Teachers' college sure was an experience. The task of mastering three rigorous years and the superb experiences can never be obliterated. Every experience had its merits, the benefits of every moment spent in college both on and off campus was one that compelled: Total divergence from all behaviors against college

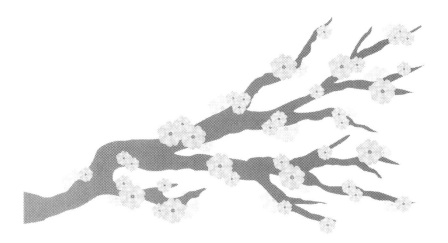

ethics, the warm embrace of diversification and culture, respect for all, empathy, transformation, and excellence.

The benefits of those years can never be adequately expressed in words. The lived experiences, the ability to impart the knowledge and the richness of the values can only be expressed with action. I received much more than I thought that I needed. I anticipated straight and simple exposure; I was however exposed to a world I never imagined.

The spirit to serve is the answer to the reason why I started my journey. This bestowed on me a magnanimous legacy for a lifetime; an answer that supersedes all answers.

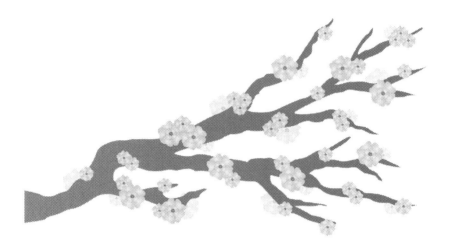

The next step

Graduation

Graduation: Like many, I did not graduate with accolades and recognized by the college like many others were. However, the day at graduation I had already accepted my accolades, when I looked back at the very child that propelled the journey and what it meant for me on that day.

That conviction! Was the greatest accolade that could have ever been given to me and the college had already made it possible from the first year in that institution. I felt that day as if I was the most coveted graduate and I had gotten the greatest Honor that any student could have received.

My sincere gratitude to all those persons who saw me through the years. I never formally thanked my mentors who were my teachers, my peers and all the academic and even ancillary staff who in their way tried to make us contented. Thank you! One and all and God, Bless you richly.

(1997-2000, ended my college years).

The Journey after Graduation

The journey continued after graduation with utmost eagerness to impart and practice much of what I learnt in college. This journey led me to the formal education system; an urban high school where I opted for the position as a guidance counselor. Being a fresh college graduate, 'can anyone imagine! How much I was rearing to flex my new-found knowledge? I had already started doing my own research on behaviors, and anticipating the great experiences that I would have with parents, teachers, and students. The numerous challenges having to serve through: Cultural differences, economic, academic, and ethnic variations, and differences.

I trusted my knowledge, training, determination, and professionalism- backed by a strong psychological understanding of most areas targeted in the education system. Those for sure that I anticipated could possibly pose innumerable social, legal, psychological, social, economic, and educational challenges. I envisaged transformation and steady growth in the process of exercising psychological awareness and importance. As I weighed in on being a Guidance Counselor, it gave

way to the thought that there was so much more that I could do if I delved deeper into Developmental Psychology and learning. This I was already exposed to but I wanted so much more.

I had a passion for the psychology of learning and for the whole business of education. I decided to go another step further and mark my word, "No one! Absolutely, no one! Understood me, no one knew what I was doing and why." Why was I not satisfied with what I had already achieved from three years of teachers' college? It was a question that rang like a bell in my ears. It came directly and indirectly. I learnt to shut out all the questions and concerns about furthering the journey of greater knowledge. I went searching for my passion. It was then that I was introduced to the International University of the Caribbean (IUC), formerly (ITLD).

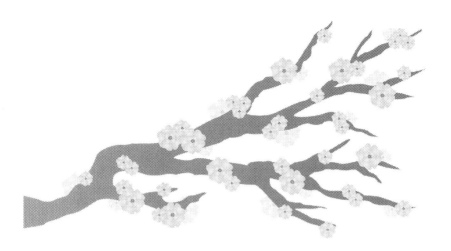

The second phase of my journey

Interestingly, after graduating teachers' college within the following year 2001, I applied to the now International University of the Caribbean (IUC) . When faced with this phase, even with the self-confidence I had, I knew that it was a challenge but! I decided that if life is a challenge why not pursue what it has to offer anyway. I learnt that challenges are no threat or defeat, unless! you fail to prepare yourself for the inevitable. Transition in any shape or form is a challenge, "Be prepared". Another portion of life's journey, I have accepted is: - (what the mind can conceive it can achieve it). I had already achieved so much of that which I could and did not even conceive. So, there we go. I was ready again.

Truth be told, the will to succeed takes the strength of the mind; the hard-core perseverance, resilience, and determination (PRD). I was already girded with my (PRD). I did my research and contacted the school. I was not as fortunate as before when I applied to Teachers College.

After the long wait, I was acknowledged and thanked for considering the institution but that they just ended the first semester and the second semester had already started and therefore; I would have to wait for the start of the new school year; which was the following year.

My attempt to pursue my goal seemed to have swiveled, my faith immediately focused the possibility not where the semester was. I called the school and I was told that I could not be accommodated and I said, "Thank you! "But", I uttered, "Before I go, may I come in and speak with the Dean?" and the person I spoke with said "you could try". That was all I needed. A foot in the doorway. Again, I said "Thank you! I will".

I went by the school the next day to speak with the Dean; the secretary was very pleasant and accommodated me in a very impressive and professional manner. Of course, I had to explain the reason for my visit and that I did. I was offered a seat and told that I may have to make an appointment if she could not accommodate me at that time. Fortunately for me the Dean Dr. Baker :-(not her real name) agreed to accommodate me.

I was warmly greeted and offered a seat. I spoke to the Dean who was responsible for the Psychology department and expressed my willingness

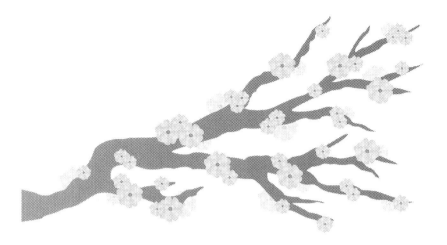

to be in the program she said I would have to wait for the next batch the following year. She went further to say that the first term had ended and they were going into the second term a student may be considered when the first term starts but not when it ends. I pleaded subtly and so positive that I knew I could do it.

I expressed the fact that I do understand however, I was confident that I would be able to manage, if I was given the opportunity to take on the challenge. She laughed and said…. You sound so sure of yourself' (I so remember the laugh and the bow of her head as she laughed) ….. "It is the start of the second term; there is no way the institution will allow that because you will never be able to catch up with what the other students have already done". She said no one has ever asked to be allowed to do that and she went further to say that I would never be able to catch up with what was going on in the course and why would I want to waste my money because she knew that I would end up failing the first year.

I remembered the daring look on her face and response that followed. I envisaged it was more of a shock to her for someone to think of taking on such a charge than a doubt in her mind about my ability. I said to her, "Dr. Baker, (not her real name) I can appreciate what you are saying however, not because you have never been approached by

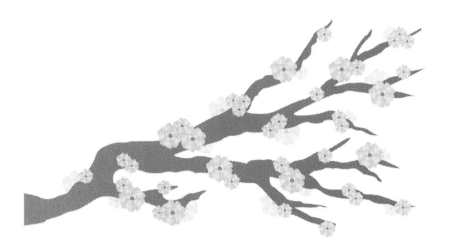

another student, it does not mean that it cannot be done. Please, give me the benefit of the doubt, I have an agenda and I know that I can, I will try my best." I told her to give me the benefit of the doubt. Please! Please! Please! I lauded. She looked at me and said, "When you lose your money do not blame us, I already told you that such an action we do not encourage, it is not a wise practice, students will blame us for their failure." She further said, "You have asked, I will grant that request but it will be on your merit". She summoned her secretary to provide me with the necessary documents that would afford me the opportunity to move forward. I was registered with a grin that I will never forget.

I was once again comfortably seated while the secretary did what she was commanded to do. She had me sign on what was necessary and engaged me in a semi- orientation as orientation was long gone from the beginning of the school year. The rest of the orientation process I was exposed to as I did the various classes throughout the weeks ahead. I was given first term's instructions and assignments. Again, no one understood why and what I was thinking and what lead me to taking such a dumb action. If I had allowed myself to be understood I sure would be confined by trying to conciliate the benefit of others. I was given the syllabus and all the course work and a specific time to cover

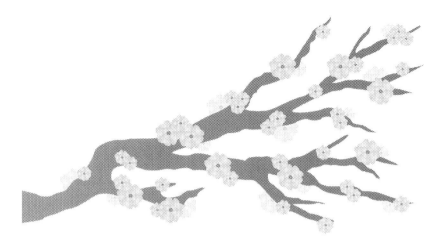

course work that had passed. When I received everything, I said all the thank you necessary and unnecessary.

I walked down the staircase from the building where all the offices were located and as I descended I could see from my mind's eye the smile on the Dean's face. From there I went to secure all that I needed for my next day.

I knew that I had taken on something that I, myself, again! Did not understand how I was going to get it done but, the determination, the resilience, and the perseverance in me with the fact that the "WORD" once again, I repeated to myself in a whisper, 'I can do all things through Christ who strengthens me.' I rested in my belief that I only had to apply myself and give it my best shot. The strength and the understanding that I gained from teachers' college gave me the strategic competitiveness, perfect play on my academic game plan and a shore shot at my target.

I understood the game but needed more to follow the academic demands going forward. I presented myself very early for my first class that afternoon. The classes were conducted at different times on various days; unlike teachers' college where I had to get there by 8: 30 am, five days per week.

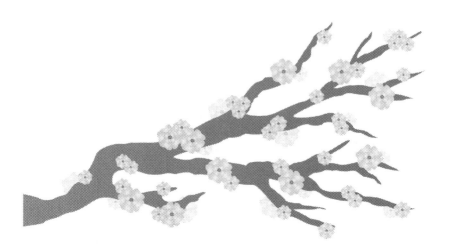

I was unemployed while attending teachers' college but for my first degree it was school and work. The challenges were numerous and many times the stressors seemed insurmountable and again the Pain-tears and simultaneously joy-tears kept coming and going. It is very hard to understand 'joy-tears' and 'pain-tears.' I knew them both. I was very humbled by these two factors; for the years through teachers' college they were my best friends. They were what I connected with most and they were what taught me; "Press on," I did psychology in teachers' college and I knew that all the parameters of emotional psychology are expressed by many emotions and sometimes none.

In many circumstances and especially in the process of transitioning, at any level emotions are usually high. Not many transitions; no matter what reason or occasion are embraced. The lecturers were very practical in pointing out the standards that guided the learning process and joining the classes later would not exclude me from what was expected.

I was not excluded from completing course work, final exams and some group work that were already in, you know what that means. I was on my own with no changes to what was expected. For a while, I was my group. Needless to say – hypothetically, courage was my backup. I took on the challenge, therefore, delivery was not an option; production was

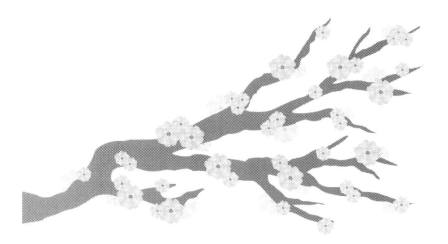

the deal and we were (myself, and my own convection) absolutely 'no excuses'- clear on that. The second semester went by with grave tension and the tacit moments were evident.

This did not go unnoticed; my instructors and simultaneously other students saw the metamorphic tacitness that was eventually expressed openly; expressed evidently by the work that was produced and the rewards that were merited. The moments through the year were less interactive than that of teachers' college. The responsibility bestowed on us as students was multifarious and time was of the essence.

We were in and out of classes and most persons were either coming from or going to work therefore, very little time was left for much student to student interaction, those moments between and after classes were spent with faculty members ensuring that we were on the right path with class assignments and preparations for exams when they are posted. Most student interactions were basically for meeting to corroborate group discussions and collaborate on projects/assignments. Neverless, we found social moments in between and brief moments after classes most group work were done in another group members office, the library or any comfortable place we could find to accommodate all group members and one conducive to working on projects.

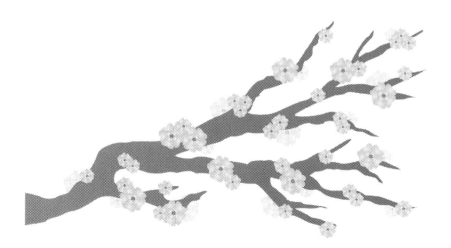

College activities were at a minimum so during this two-year period most of the academic and social energy were concentrated on getting the work done. Class sessions were exciting as I delved more into the psychology of learning and development. These were some of the most interesting times in the learning process, very intense and overtly challenging as catching up was a bit of a 'concentration – overdrive' that had to be in motion every step of the way.

Catching up and getting on was indeed an intense trajectory, however, the crave for this knowledge was so fulfilling as the understanding of psychologists like Piaget's as the Developmental Psychology Journal accentuate the scientific study of changes in human development from infancy adolescence adult and beyond. It was a very serious and compelling period in my quest for some of the changes described in the journal: Moral understanding, social change, personality, emotional development, self-concept, and identity-formation. Having this knowledge gave me the power to act with preciseness, understanding and urgency with utmost patience.

The knowledge empowered me with the necessary skills that helped me to identify eagerness and unease in my own child and how to combat those emotions. I noted very well the similarity and differences

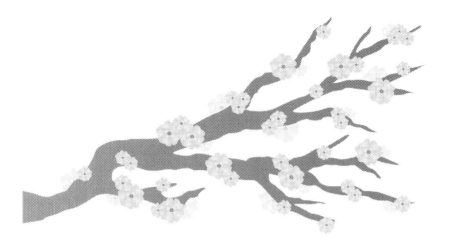

in psychological factors. I paid keen attention to studies from the great movers and shakers of Psychology such as: Erikson, Freud, Vygotsky, Burner, Kohlberg, Jugg, Watson, Bandura; these psychologists were indeed some of my favorites. The Behavioral and Cognitive Psychology at this level as noted by the American Board of Professional Psychology engaged research, education training and practices.

This speaks true to the approach and level of psychology that I was exposed to in my Counseling Psychology classes which were my main focus. Again, as noted by the American Board of Professional Psychology (ABP), this area of Psychology deals with: Individuals, groups, and community which evidently takes in the responsibility of counselors to look at the emotional, behavioral, vocational, and mental health problems. No psychological concern and outward behavior would go unnoticed, observation became a part of me both at Home and school.

As a Guidance Counselor and especially being in the classroom, it was imperative and I again mention the American Board of Professional Psychology (ABP), and numerous other psychology bearing texts noted that the required actions necessary for the profession as a guidance counselor they included: Preventative interventions, developmental and remedial approaches, assessments, diagnosis, and treatment.

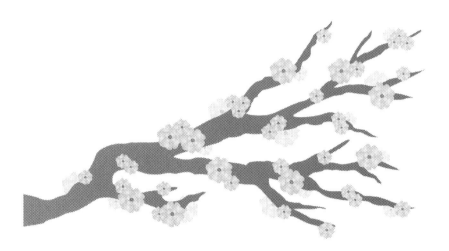

I was blessed with some of the best who taught these subject areas. It was such a pleasure for me as I absorbed the importance of analyzing various cases and what makes the difference in the lives of individuals. My moment of proverbial tell-all reaction from my own child and my initial inability; had me on the proverbial search. I simplistically recognized my own response to the psychological jab that was only expressed as a seemingly lost parent in the wild. I fervently searched for answers, reasons and even sympathy.

As the learning of Psychology cushioned my passion and understanding, I dare to coin my own version and meaning of a behavior and I state: - {one's behavior is just a reaction to the circumstances encountered hitting on the psychological zone causing immediate or delayed actions; be it voluntary or involuntary, satisfactory to the psychological jab experienced}.

Interestingly! As intrigued as I was about my ability to comprehend much of the behaviors scientifically assessed by psychologists, I was convinced that my personal experience was an isolated one. Isolated, because everything seemed surreal, the support that surrounded the child seemed perfect.

Yet! Her behavior created the root which a mother held onto and inculcated a moment of truth to a journey unimagined by many.

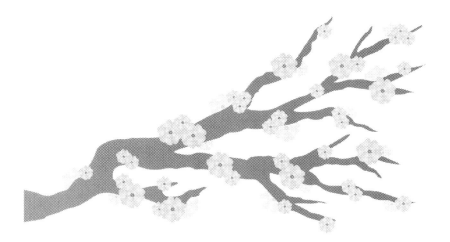

The root of this magnificent tree did not start from my vision but from an innocent involuntary creation that was voluntarily caught. This scenario was 'the tentaculation of my senses going after targets' with the hope in mind to allow for the manifestation of a satisfying need to be fulfilled; for many to understand much more about keen observation and action. My response was a reaction to the circumstance that caught me clueless.

I pondered many times the clueless unimagined progression that I challenged. Was I beaten by conscience, reflex action, hurt, curiosity. The ponderansity continued to stretch my imagination into both the 'here and now and where from here,' even though I had completed teachers' college, I never stop asking the questions. 1. Am I truly here? 2. What next and will I make it? 3. If only for the satisfaction of one child's discomfort, why all this higher education challenge? 4. is this for self-actualization or is it out of frustration? 5. Am I trying to get something important across to those who take serious matters too lightly and ignore the core element in the obvious?

As I progressed with my classes and as mentioned in the former paragraph, I kept asking myself what kind of response psychology would affix to the result of my "Tree."

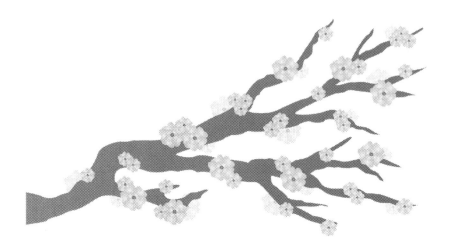

"Would this be Classical Conditioning as the psychologist Pavlov described it to be reflexive /automatic learning where the stimulus evokes the response?" I was not sure, or, maybe; I was forced to act or my action was an automatic one. I went back into my thoughts and seemingly by reason of understanding psychological responses/behavior, I pondered whether it was Operant Conditioning, again, another of Pavlov's explanation to one's psychological response.

I asked myself the question "Is this the eye opener, am I teaching a lesson or am I learning a lesson? My academic journey started with a question. Where do I turn and to whom do I turn? The significance of a root problem gave me the first idea that from the root if ignored dries up and dies. If attention is given it will survive and grow. The important thing is "What do you envision while you nourish this root? As the old - adage goes; there are so much more questions than answers. I have no answers I just state the facts. I was ravaged with uncertainty and quickly realized that the result of uncertainty would only leave me ravaged, I moved in the direction of being certain about making a significant difference to the journey I had embarked for the benefit of all who needed this lesson and for those who will read my book.

Third Voyage

After graduating with my Bachelors in Guidance Counseling, the tree sprang a new branch which forced its way into administrative and leadership responsibilities. I was exposed to numerous options to peruse my education at the Masters level. Once again, the questions, concerns, challenges; in numerous shapes and forms came thunderously at me because no one understood me. I was seen as an unreasonable and an uncontrolled selfish bookworm. To most, my motive was not clear. Well! Maybe it was not very clear to me either, however, I kept hanging on and nourishing the tree as I surmised and thought let the tree prosper. A,ha! Low and behold, I did my research on various institutions for all the information that I needed about the Master's program. I took on the challenge and went through the connections of the Sam Sharpe Teachers' College that I attended to educate myself about an oversees Masters program that was offered at the time.

The college was the surrogate for this oversees institution and based on the information from my research, they were satisfactory. I took the next step by submitting an application to Central Connecticut State

University as requested and anxiously awaited a response. While I waited, I earnestly kept the prayers going and I will admit that flicking my fingers almost became a habit as anxiety weighed in with the thought of how I intended to support this gigantic move.

I wrestled long and hard with the possibility and the impossibility, I kept weighing both until they seemed to merge into what I was confronted with. "My reason," I looked at where it all started and wondered how far my search for help was taking me. I needed no answers or went in search of any; of any sort, I just knew that the branches from the "Tree" were spreading and I just had to hold on to my tree. The initial classes for the oversees Master's program started at the Teachers' College and we were graced with some of the finest professors that you could imagine. It was a two-year Educational Leadership program which had to be completed on campus in Connecticut. Classes were very intense and there was no room for anything but serious work and total dedication to the challenge, the grades had to be kept at the highest level in order to move from one level to the other.

Despite the rigorous schedule, there were light moments to which the professors engaged the students into discussions that somewhat leveled the educational field; the boundary would be lifted for those

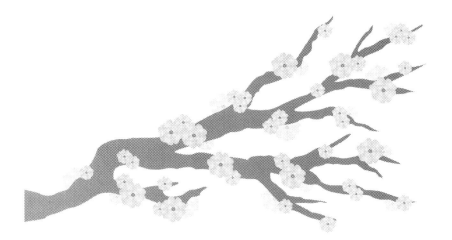

moments. They would start by saying "Hey! Guys just take time to look at where you are, what motivated us all? Where we had broad discussions on who we really are and notably in the discussions; what we genuinely represented, our whys, our dreams, aspirations and in many instances challenges on the journey.

One professor Dr. Lori made the entire class laughed uncontrollably, she was always jovial and most times lightened the moments, and she gave us synapses of how she became who she was. Dr. Lori related to the class how proud she was to be who she became and how much she was inspired by those who taught her. For me, every moment was an inspiration; I had embarked on a journey that must accredit to the force behind it.

Deep in my mind and as the goodly Psychologist would explain – it, 'deep,' came from deep in my sub consciousness; my superego, to my ego and overtly into my id so that it could be expressed. I was eager to find the help that was desired to address the cry of one child and furthermore knowing that the answer to one child's concerns would also be the answer to many. Classes were exciting and very intense, I had very caring and supportive classmates, my dearest friends were Chris, Rosemarie, and Olga, who were like real family.

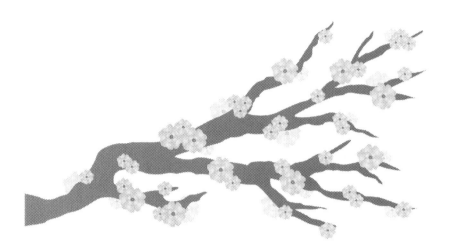

Chris was the comedian in the group and when we were heavily pressured he would make our moments so much lighter especially when he gave the stories about his dogs. The stories he told were so funny - every day before and after classes his stories alone would help to allay all fears and stress of the classes. The two years in the program between Jamaica and Connecticut were two marvelous years. The campus setting in Jamaica was a familiar one as the main stay was the teachers' college that I had previously attended. The period on the campus in Connecticut was a marvelous experience, the grandiose buildings, and the generous staff from grounds men to the President on the campus one could not ask for a more professional and welcoming group of people.

The campus environment made me feel so much comfort, totally relaxed and fully facilitated, so much so that the classes and the learning process seemed heavily subsidized with comfort. The wide expanse of the campus was busy with students going to and from classes, books, computers, cell phones… you name them – could be seen lying all around on benches. The secured setting was one of the many pictures that never left my mind. It showed that discipline was never compromised.

I felt honored as a student to be a part of such an institution and learnt in no uncertain manner the importance of leadership. As a student of

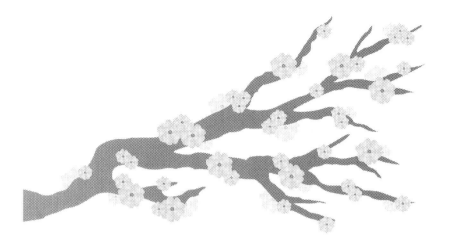

Psychology, it proved the scientific understanding of Kolb's Experimental Learning Theory where he notes that the holistic perspectives combined experience, perception, cognition, and behavior. The same concept of learning as applies by Dewey also one of my favorites that I studied. In the leadership study, numerous kinds and levels were observed, however, the psychology of leadership and leadership practices hold true to how you lead, how much and what you learn from these leaders and ultimately what kind of leader one intends to be.

I was ready for any challenge, teachers' college gave me the platform with my audience, Psychology gave me the understanding and the ideas and Leadership taught me how to lead. Every day I walked the corridors, the campus and before I walk into the classrooms, I thought to myself that the leadership of this institution is truly an honorable leader, there was so much poise and grace and professionalism in every conceivable area of the campus and not to mention the décor and order of the physical structures. I remarked time and time again what better place to learn what constitutes effective leadership and administrative responsibilities. I saw myself as an effective, efficient, proud, and affable leader rearing to go.

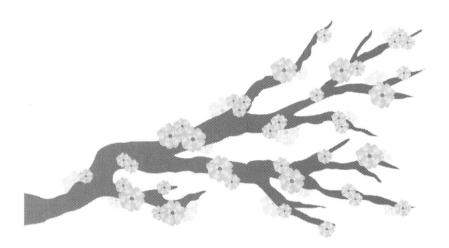

With all the experiences that I gleaned, I kept looking back at my why, I recognized that a child's anguish and lack of adult misunderstanding and simultaneously the lack of the adult misunderstanding of a child-created the manifestation of that root, the root that I acknowledged and held onto; had fed the growth of an educational tree that I never could have imagined.

If I had failed to listen and not to act, I would have lost a child's intellectual ability, I would have not realized a dream that I thought was virtually impossible, I would have lost the experience and the opportunity to serve others. To observe analyze and make the right choice to hold on. Hold on! Hold on! Hold on. I shared my story with many and so too my professors and colleagues on the campus. Every lecture and every assignment I say my 'why' and my 'is this really me.' I buried my consciousness into the one day I will prove it attitude I was still waking up to my transformation.

The experience was priceless and the challenges at times seemed insurmountable, but then, we really bonded as a group and encouraged each other, sleepless nights as usual that was a norm throughout the learning Process. I persevered as I was always determined to make it through to the end. The trepidation came with the examination

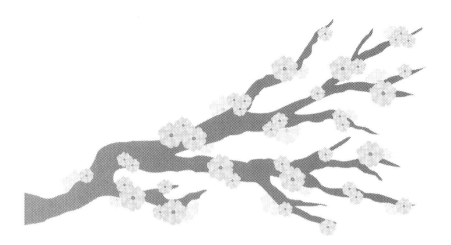

preparations again the hallmark of learning. We formed study groups but unfortunately for me I was not very good at group studying, group assignments I do my share and corporate fully, not a problem however exam preparations, I had to be in a corner. Ha! May be strange but silence did it. I graduated and went back into the thick of teaching and training, helping others to be the best that they can be. No regrets.

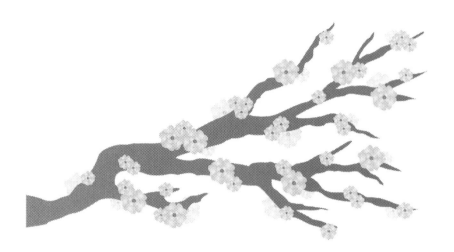

A great wish

To conduct an interview with:

Some key persons who inspired me so that I could have them create a Page in my first book. They have already created my academic success and that indelible rank will always remain.

❖ Dr. Cecile former principal of the Sam Sharp Teachers' College where I pursued a Diploma in Education. She encouraged me to do a major in Guidance and Counseling which was the best decision that I made at the time. It netted the purpose of my journey and answered all my questions and concerns that took me there.

❖ Dr. Clarke, from the International University of the Caribbean where I pursued my degree. She believed in me and gave me the opportunity to realize my academic dream and also afforded me

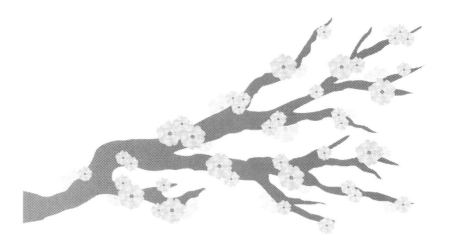

the answers to my questions through the exposure and teaching that they provided.

❖ Dr. Lorie, from Central Connecticut State University where I pursued my Masters Degree. Dr. Lori related to the class on numerous occasions how proud she was to be who she became and how much she was inspired by those who taught her. She assured us that no matter what and how great the challenge is - strive to succeed, never allow the challenge to override the path to success.

❖ Dr. Mitchell, former Dean of Argosy University. When I thought that all was lost and my academic dream was in shambles, he never gave up on me and he never at anytime encouraged me to feel sorry for myself or to even think that I could not make it. He guided me and never cease to hammer it home in my head that I must not look behind keep going the horizon is just my effort away just put it in.

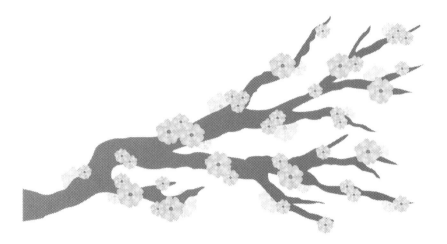

❖ Dr. Larry, from Argosy University where I pursued my Doctoral studies. Some professors are like stars in the sky where they shine bright, make you smile and give you the assurance that no height is too high and no light is too bright that you cannot outshine. She is one to make you feel that you are always at that place where reaching for the star is only your effort away. There is an extraordinary inspirational tone in her daily guiding words that sets the pace for nothing outside of success.

For myself, all I needed was help to address the cry of one child. I am often extremely mesmerized by the golden opportunity that I have been afforded just by paying close attention to a child's silent plea. I wondered to myself at every chance I get, how many mothers have been moved by a child for whatever reason. How many roots have withered or better yet how many roots have been nourished and cherished because of the silent plea of one small child. How many! How many!

Voyage Four

After I graduated with a Master of Science Degree, from Central Connecticut State University, I evaluated the mission and vision of my 'why'. By then I was travelling extensively and making many strides; not even sure how purpose full some of them were. Again, as fate would have it the

The opportunity came to my door where pursuing a doctoral degree as the final step would complete the journey that had started that glorious August morning in 1997.

Once again, I jumped at the opportunity and naturally to the surprise of many. Thank God! for my children who even when they do not understand why; they believed in me. I took on the challenge and I ran with it after I did my research and was satisfied with what was offered at Argosy University. Once again, I applied to the university as was the normal procedure, I waited with bated breath which again was the normal procedure, I was more seasoned to the institution's processes and was less anxious about the outcome.

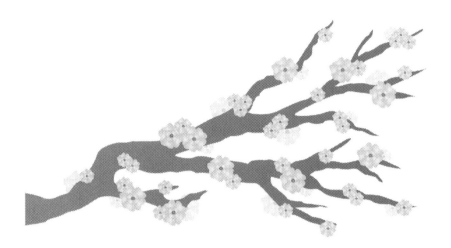

I was notified a few weeks after that I needed to submit a paper stating my reasons for choosing Argosy University, why I had an interest in pursuing a doctoral degree, how and what I intend to do in order to ensure a successful completion. I had to find every means and reasons to convince the relevant authority that I was the right candidate for their institution. It was a very tall order and I was deeply impressed knowing that it was stated in no uncertain terms that hard work was the hallmark of the journey. It was clearly stated that all requirements must be met in order for any consideration to be given to applicants.

I thanked God, that I satisfied all the university's requirements. I was finally instructed to write an essay which would further satisfy other criteria and so I did. I knew that there would be another waiting period in the making and I was prepared for that period with all optimism. It was late November and moving into the month of December when I became a bit curious and I called the school because I remembered that the orientation would commence before the January semester. I proceeded to make the connection with the school's student services department with the expectation to - as usual, get answers. I was directed to the academic counselor to whom I gave my information.

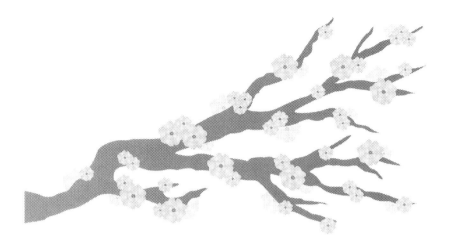

She was surprised when I told her that I was not informed about orientation. 'I may not have followed the instructions carefully,' I admitted. Even though I got an acceptance letter I guess I was waiting to be further instructed. Maybe that was quite silly of me. She surprisingly made a few shouts in disbelief 'What! Where have you been'? Now I was shocked and I asked her what she meant by that. To my amazement, she said the professor informed her that one student did not show up for orientation. I dangled my feet a bit as I felt the nerves tingling and patience jabbing at my side. I said to her, 'How could I be a part of your orientation that I was not aware of? She hastily told me to get on to the professor because two weeks of orientation had passed and the first-class assignment was due. Another challenge of the same fate that I encountered; missing out on a previous orientation once before and now having to catch up on assignments.

I in my meekness and strong – faith, I just lifted my eyes and said 'Lord! as usual, I seek Your Guidance going forward.' I was in constant dialogue with my academic counselor who from the beginning was very accommodating and never cease to be supportive. I was told how to get into the Campus Commons and how to find my way around; I fumbled around quite a bit as this was an area completely foreign to me.

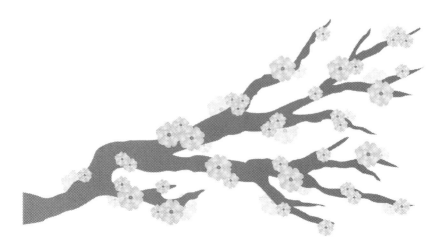

I made a second call to my academic counselor and she guided me through to the classroom and where to find the professor for the course I was about to take as well the first assignment. With much anticipation, I eagerly familiarized myself with my new environment and wondered about my ability to manage online to such a great extent.

My curiosity calmed my gut wrenching nerve and that calmness sailed me through to what I was not totally prepared for. With no escape route, I paddled and ploughed my way through like a kayak being guided down the river by strong men with anxiety written across the brow on their faces. I was that image and more. I had no time to speculate or procrastinate time was of the essence. I had to hit the ground running. Some of the most serious times were ahead of me and that I certainly recognized and never at any time took a moment for granted. I was on a mission to fulfill a need.

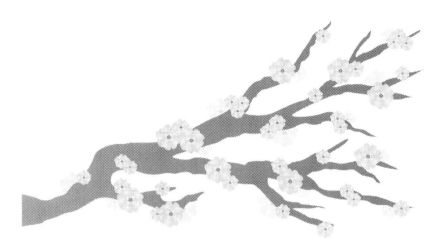

The Real Challenge

The Online Classroom

I ventured into the unknown, I was totally oblivious to an online classroom, the struggle I had getting to find the Campus Commons was one, getting into it was two, finding the professor's instructions and class notes was three, finding the work to be done after the notes and instructions was four, responding to the professor and asking questions was five and last, but not least number six was submitting the work for the professors to vet and reply or give a grade.

Quoting from (Bergquist & Pawlak, 2008) the 'tangible culture' that I was accustomed to throughout the learning process conversely, had changed primarily from face- to- face interaction and auditory to a more diverse perspective of institutional territorial extended learning (I TE L) which is my interpretation of Online Learning (OL).

I fumbled mercilessly around what I was introduced to as the Campus Commons. My first month was a nightmare, I was already behind, I dazzled and dazed and mumbled and fumbled my way in and

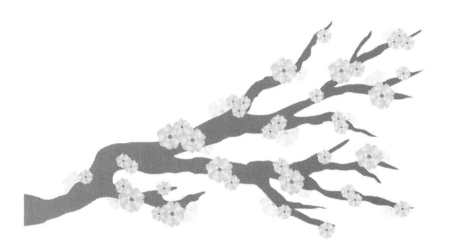

around the Campus Commons (CC). I realized after the first month that I had even missed the notices and some instructions posted by my very first professor. There was a penalty for doing so but Lucky for me I was able to somehow avoid most with the help of my academic counselor. She helped me to explain my way out of the penalty for not following instructions knowing that the fault was squarely at my feet but it was not out of negligence it was a genuine mistake on my part. The crucial part that I suffered was the assignment and class discussion pile up. Getting those done was not an option, that I could not escape. There was no help, no pardon, nor was there any excuse for that part of the deal it had to be done.

I tried crying many times but I realized that I needed the clear eyes and total absence of tears to see and focus on the workload. Tears would only be a hindrance so I aborted the need to do so. Hard work, dedication and selflessness propelled the process day after day. For the first semester, I had no time to process the realistic academic dynamites that were awaiting me for the rest of the term. I just buried myself into the pile that I was expected to get through within the specified time.

I felt like begging for mercy, but! Where would I go for that, I chided softly to myself. Only a sigh would normally follow that

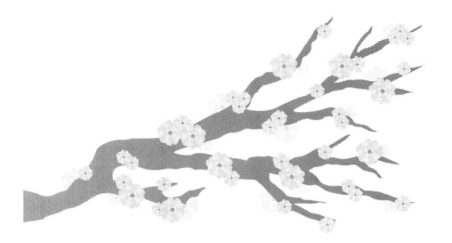

generous thought of seeking mercy; which I really thought I needed at the time. Working online for me was unconventional. I was deeply challenged as I was not a computer whiz and more over I was competing with those who were. I tried not to focus too much on those matters, I depended more on getting the work done and to seek the necessary means of getting my professors attention. I actively participated in class discussions which I had to do at least three days per week, liaising with technical support, and close contact with my counselor.

The first semester, the second, and the third were no less tedious. I had such a struggle that at the end of it all I wanted to hibernate for a year. During the break, I wondered to myself what on earth I had gotten myself into, but then, I asked myself the obvious question. Doesn't everyone with all intention and purpose finish what they start? And again, who told me that it would be easy anyway. I laughed at myself many times in the process and ended up feeling foolish.

For the first few years, I did no travelling but the seminars and the webinars and the host of notes and information to process. Yes! the professors polled every stop and made no bones about gathering information analyzing scholarly material, assessing other students posts and participating in class discussions. All written material, verbal

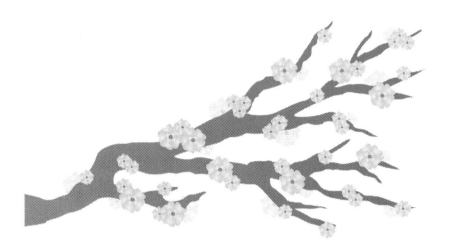

presentations and comments regarding responses to other students' classroom postings had to include references if they were not our own words; not sometimes all the time. Plagiarism was such as serious offence that no mistake could be made at any time regarding any work produced by us as students. Reading and analyzing became one of my chores. Daily assessment and discussions of material produced by scholars took every fiber of my thought process and analytical knowledge. To read widely was like regular meals throughout the days and months; all scholarly books and as a matter of fact, all print and electronic material along with their instructions and information required careful analysis when reported in class discussions and assignments.

It was all read, read, read, and more reading. That was no joke. After the first year, I was fired up. I was rearing to go more than ever, and then came the second and the third after the third year I knew that my brain was saying there is space but I could not find it. I was so cluttered and dragged and exhausted and physically drained. I pulled myself up and tried to stay focus on my 'why' as I looked at when I started and I looked at where I was.

The first year was like the seatbelt in a vehicle; it held me so close to the doctoral seat that despite the rigors of it all I felt firm in the position.

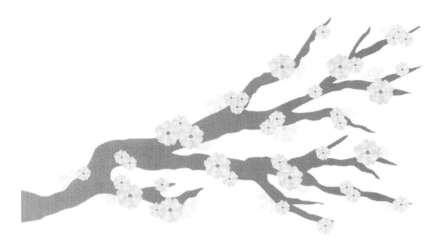

After the first three years, had passed, I knew that I could not turn back so I pressed on, I cannot say how I made it to three because words will not permit me to express the self-sacrifice. By then I was left without social, physical, emotional, and not to mention financial stability.... I pressed on anyway.

All I knew and could recognize was what and how learning at the highest level was taught and acquired. I was confronted with numerous academic and psychological hurricanes on my journey I remembered clearly that looking back was not on my watch. Law governing education, statistics, budgeting, and curriculum design were three of the greatest challenges that I had. I failed my first statistics course and I am not afraid or ashamed to disclose this. I need others to understand that failure is when you give in to the unethical will to retreat when you are knocked down. The idea is to get on your feet and keep moving.

I could have stayed down but I would not be able to go where there is no path and furthermore to leave a positive trail. I tried harder the next time around, I had to do the entire course all over and could not fail. I made it the second time around many did not make it thus far so I am truly grateful. The work was such a challenge that many times I told myself it was time to give up. I saw so many of my colleagues walk

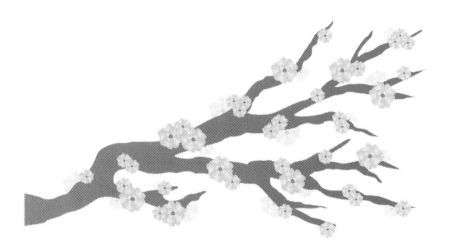

away it was painful, some made it through to the first few years and said that was it, they preferred to go sane than to challenge how much more it would take them to go insane.

Some got to final exam term and did not make it. The preparation alone for final exams was a nerve wreck many could not even take exams the stress alone made some people sick the few who did, some were still left behind. I thanked God for helping me through it all and as I stated earlier, no words can describe the sacrifice and stresses that I encountered over those years.

Research was like a shot gun you keep shooting until you hit the target, research methods confused so many of us that we were convinced we would not live to conquer the course or get to where we would be able to conduct one. I was blessed with one of the greatest experts in my final research year and I survived. I did not only complete my research but I was able to create my own theory (G.A.P.) in the system. I will continue to conduct my own research at a later date. I intend to utilize the findings from this research to enhance research methods and the curriculum design knowledge that I already gained from this program. Education has been my passion and will continue to be.

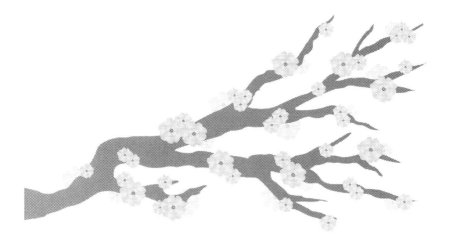

I recognized a world that was ignited by the concerns for a child who needed help. One who was too young to understand the struggle of her own mother as she tried to find the answer to her woes and had no thought of controlling how far I would go or even imagined that I would have gone. It is such a marvelous and truly an ironic situation never at any time after leaving high school did I even consider the word college more so to attempt applying to one. As a student, I was deprived of many things, however, I made a promise to my child that I had to find the answer to her unease. I thought I found it after attending Sam Sharp Teachers' College and graduated as a Guidance Counselor but then I went two steps further. I imagined that by my own admonition against settling for less my determination kept me travelling the academic journey.

The road was not easy and as the song says never an ending. Yet, 'It is a rough road that leads to the heights of greatness' (Brainy Quote). My educational journey taught me that: Truly the race is not for the swift, I have endured, I persevered through to the end of my doctoral studies. evidently:

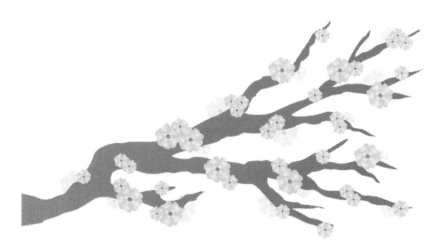

Heights of great men reach and kept were not attained by sudden flight but they while their companion slept were toiling upward through the night.
(Henry Wadsworth)

Through it all there were weeks, and months, when my days followed my days i.e. (I never knew nights), I did forget many times that I had a place to sleep. Why? my nights were treated as regular daytime. I never had that luxury of sleep; for weeks and months. All levels of learning were tedious and exigent tasks, they demanded so much that selflessness was the only choice through it all. I have been there. 'Chuckle' here and there was a part of the study and assignment routine. Ha! Came in very handy. Wouldn't you think? Yes! It did. Sleepless nights in pursuit of the doctoral journey was just one of the many prices that I proudly paid to have listened to my child and nourished the root that she created; with her own challenge. I held on to my 'TREE' that grew from that root. The midnight light. was my sunlight as the sun was always shining, nighttime was not on the

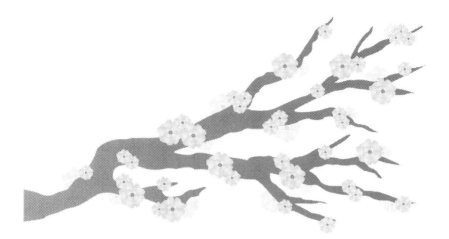

agenda. I am very proud to say that mission has been accomplished and I am here to serve; not to be served.

We all have our 'Why's' and our purpose which must be recognized, and generated according to our skills, abilities, and potential. Let us act now for the service of our fellowmen.

Travelling

My academic journey took me through life's hills and valleys. I swam the high seas of distress, yet still I have no regrets. I caved in many times when my back was against the walls of what next, yet still I have no regrets, I ran a race that was not in my repertoire, yet still I have no regrets. I was required to do a fair amount of travelling throughout the six plus years in my doctoral studies. From time to time I travelled to Atlanta and Texas for group and one to one work sessions with professors.

Travelling was one aspect of this journey that taught me toughness, humility and what it meant to go beyond any boundary that appears to be a deterrent. The airport chairs were my resting place many nights on many occasions. I never complained as I had a goal in mind and refused to allow any challenge/s to compromise my journey, much of my sacrifices will be a shock to many as I never complained about the numerous disadvantages that I encountered. I was more low keyed, humbled, and grateful to God for seeing me through.

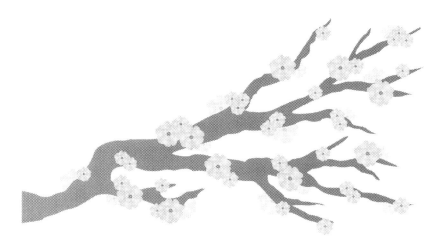

I am grateful to all those persons who have opened their doors to me and encouraged me along the way. Strong Tower provided me a secure church home and a spiritual family that can never be forgotten. My sincere gratitude to each and every one who held my hand spoke kind words and wished me well. This helped to make my journey lighter. The support of all those who taught me directly and indirectly I am truly and will always remain grateful for their input, they made me who I am now. All the encouragements and even the discouragement they all strengthened and enlightened me.

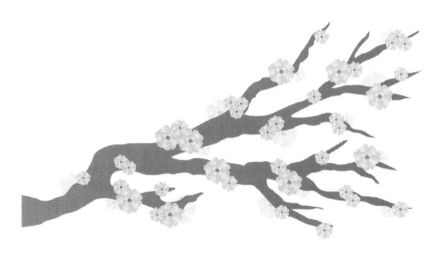

Words

Ponderosity – heaviness: - noun (www.thesarus)

Stultified – impede, frustrating means, degrade (Dictionary.com)

'Child-Misunderstanding Syndrome' - Risk factor of a child not understanding an adult response

Adult- Misunderstanding Syndrome'- - Risk factor of an adult not understanding a child's responds

Capricious – unpredictable (Dictionary.com)

Oxymoron: Figure of speech with contradictory words

Rhetorical – ascension: an unexpected answer to a continuous question that is constantly moving to the surface (C. Kellier, 2017)

Chatoyant: To change luster

Exigent: Critical, needing immediate attention

Roots - source or origin of something

Challenge - something new and different which requires great effort and determination

Inspiration - Divine influence or action.....power to move intellect or emotions

Aspiration - Hope or ambition to achieving something

Purpose - the reason for which something is done

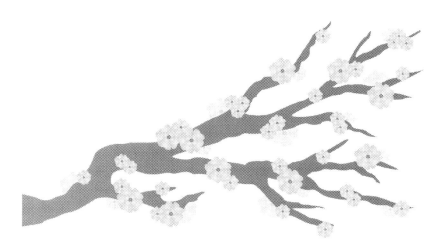

Who is Claudia E. Kellier

I consider myself an introvert but! I am 100% a people person; non-judgmental and receptive, with the conviction that I must strive to maintain the qualities that are in keeping with the Will of my Creator. I possess many qualities as described by Psychologist Carl Jug, and carefully documented by Susan Cain, such as: Being drawn to the inner world of thoughts and feeling with greater focus on meanings. My nature is one that generates positive energy, I enjoy lone time, and I am happy to note that I am immune to the lures of wealth and fame. I am a good listener, non-judgmental, expresses myself undeniably more comfortable writing than I do verbally.

As further described so amiably by Cain, Conflict is not in my path, a bit shy however; fear is never an option as I can also state categorically- that in my quest for any of life's options or challenges there is no fear factor as I am not defined by challenges. Being a wife, mother, grandmother, aunt, Educator, Author, Researcher, and Mentor; I endeavor to do my best at all times. A Christian, who thinks

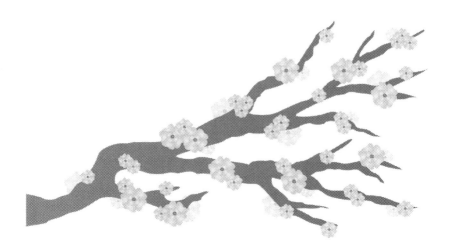

highly of God's Creation, regardless of outward appearance and inward choices.

My philosophy is: "Helping others to bring out the best in themselves at all times."

Thanks
God Bless.

Author's Mission:

To awake the consciousness of PARENTS;
EDUCATORS; LEARNERS; that learning is
reciprocative and success is found in many places
Keep the eyes fixed on success by accepting the source.

Author's Vision:

To Expand the scope of EDUCATION

References

Cain, S. (2012) Quit the Power of Introvert by
BrainyQuotes>henrywadsw129800

Classical Conditioning Learning Theories

https://www.learning-theories.com>class

https://books.google.com>education>administration>general

The Holy Bible

https://scattredquotes.com

Google-Dictionary Definition Vocabulary.com

CollinsDictionary>dictionary

googledictionary.com

Dictionary.com>browse>aspiration

C. Kellier (2017)

Winston Simplified Dictionary Advanced Edition

(https//: www.merriam-webster.com)

Census.gov>educ>educ_attai….

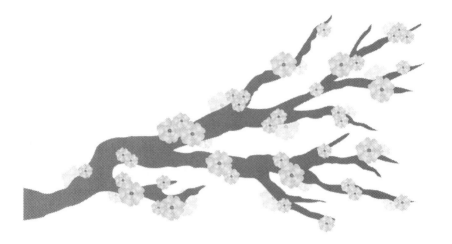

Learn

Live

Laugh

Printed in the United States
By Bookmasters